Thank you so much for praying for me. It has meant so much spiritually and emotionally as I think back on our time together and each word you spoke. The last two weeks have been extremely painful so my doctor decided to do an occipital nerve block at the base of my skull. I am getting some relief.

Praise God!

Many Thanks,
Lynn

KATHRYN'S CROSSING

A Journey to a Bridge in Africa

Lynn Brendlen

Kathryn's Crossing
A Journey to a Bridge in Africa

ISBN 978-1-935125-09-9

Printed in the United States of America

To order additional books, go to:
www.RP-Author.com/Brendlen

All proceeds from this sale of this book are donated to:
Bridging the Gap ~ Africa
410 N. Dunbridge Rd.
Bowling Green, Ohio USA 43402
www.bridgingthegapafrica.org

Robertson Publishing
59 N. Santa Cruz Avenue, Suite B
Los Gatos, California 95030 USA
(888) 354-5957 · www.RobertsonPublishing.com

Dedication

This book is dedicated to my Aunt Betty who is a sterling example of someone who lost her first daughter, her husband, and then her second daughter, yet triumphed over this pain. Her feet firmly grounded in Christ, she stands tall through life's hardest trials.

To my mother Catherine who raised three children alone with an amazingly selfless, positive attitude. Life was not about having things but about creating lasting memories. She instilled in me a zeal for adventure.

My last dedication is to the beautiful, hard-working women of Kenya. Never have I been near a group of women that I have admired more.

Acknowledgements

I am forever grateful for the loving support my husband has given me over the last forty years of marriage. He has always told me, "Lynn, you can do anything."

Thank you to my family and friends who have encouraged me in my creative abilities.

I am indebted to Harmon and Teri Parker for opening their hearts and home to me in Kenya. Without them I would never have experienced the wonder of East Africa.

Thank you to Katie Isaacs, whom I've known since she was born, for her great job in the first editing of Kathryn's Crossing.

Finally, this book could never have been birthed without the talent, creativity and insight of Molly Morris. Thank you Molly, for your skill in editing and all of your thoughtful comments and ideas.

Prologue: Africa

Intrigued, my heart as much as my rational mind hears the allure of her seductive call as if it came from the brush of a lovers lips whispering in the ear. Intimacies at their best; the words, her images, were meant for no one but me. For Africa bids me like the ocean. The sight of her from afar is so tempting — an unsailed sea of vastness wedded to the sun-dulled horizon. I am drawn down to the sandy shore, no strength or will to resist her calming earthy beauty; flirtatious waves bounce up a spray, sweet yet salty on the lips. Africa, one cannot see far enough to imagine what lies beneath her surface. One might spend a lifetime of exploration to realize it is only the opening of a door. The first step of my journey has begun.

I'm determined to walk in a new way, to travel a path I've never known. Like a toddler who is shaky, wobbling from side to side, I venture into the unfamiliar. Precariously, I take my first step into an adventure reported to be filled with danger and thrills.

Shall I leave the security and comfort of my home and community? Shall I venture out, stretch myself, fall, learn and experience the lives of others? How far will curiosity and love carry me? I stand up and set my heart toward the mystery of Africa. Her sandy beach and ocean waves await.

PART I: AFRICA CALLS TO US

My friend in the truest sense, his loyalty never wavering, proven by the most trying times, supports and warms me to the marrow. As if transported to the granite boulders heated by the Sierra summer sun, my back laying against a strength that melts away my tension. After thirty five years of marriage, he is my landscape. For when I look into his thick gray hair still turned with persistent curls at the end, I see the gray of rock, the streak of clouds woven white. The shine of vitality is there. Herbert: a name I say is ill-fitted for his persona. I'd rather call him by his second name, Ridgley, aristocratic, English and French by heritage.

In spirit, he is an Indian scout running the ridge, always on the precipice of life. While his bark-brown eyes highlighted with a rim of rich yellow are on alert—never to miss the sight of beauty. He is forever in search of a new trail, to conquer the unknown, a hunter, a seeker, a man who has taken me places I never dreamed of going. These places span the continents of the earth and reach inward to free the secret wishes that women dream of being fulfilled. So I say to myself, "My lover and I are off to Africa." The very sound of it gives me pleasure.

Only two days until fall officially starts, yet the leaves have begun to change color due to a very dry summer. Our backs turn on California's autumn hues, our family and friends, the sweet companionship of our Bischon, Itsi Bitsi, and the safety of our home. I know deep within me that our courted garden—the lush green of our lily pads

1

floating in our peaceful pond, the porch swing—this place of meditation situated in the heart of affluent Saratoga will never look the same to me again. I know the shocking volt of revelation awaits me as does the blinding sunlight when one steps out of a cave. I've prepared myself, but am I ready to see another culture with my heart? The answer seems to be yes. I'm filled with abandoned glee to embrace the unknown, the startlingly different ways of others, and the wonder of another nation.

Our plan is to stay four days in London and then fly to Nairobi, Kenya to visit friends and build a footbridge in west Pokot in honor of my cousin, Kathryn, who died only four months ago. She inspires us to reach out to others by her life of selflessness. From Nairobi, we're off for a two week private hiking and photography safari in Tanzania. After the lodges and tent camping in the bush, we'll head across the Tanzanian plains in an eight hour, off-road excursion to visit the Hadza people, a remote nomadic tribe that lives above the Yaeda Valley. A flight takes us back to Nairobi for a few days, a week in Mombasa, on the east African coast, back to Nairobi to regroup, then London for four days, then home. It's almost two months of travel. The unknown is before us, the winds of fate blow freely, the hand of God directing them.

Herb, my ambassador of charm, is already in conversation with the young man who sits next to us. The blond young man of Polish descent is leaving San Francisco business negotiations to return to London where his new bride, an attorney, awaits him. It's no surprise his firm has sent him. His charming demeanor and good looks almost overpower his quick mind. We've found out that two months ago he honeymooned in Kenya and he let us know it wasn't the most relaxing way to spend a honeymoon. At first a bit proper, he now talks of life, most likely unaware that Herb's love of people, his genuine interest in them, has unlocked his inhibitions. Some lift a glass of wine to salute the cook and say "Bon Appetit, Enjoy!" My husband ingests conversation. He reaches right in to see if he can touch the spirit of a person. This search to know others is his favorite meal.

We've taken Excedrin PM to sleep on the night flight. Now over, we wait outside in a groggy mist of fog mixed with medication at 6:00 am. We are two of many waiting for the next dark, hump-backed beetle taxi to take us to our destination. At last, our turn has come. Bleary-eyed, half here, half back in California, I can still recognize that the overweight cab driver persistently stares ahead while he pretends he doesn't know where the Paddington Best Western Hotel is. The hotel is only four blocks away and he has waited in line for a big fare. We're the bad poker hand he's drawn. Herb insists he must know where the hotel is and hands him the address. In icy silence, as if he has been refused his morning cup of tea, he drives us to the hotel. I could never identify him in a line-up for not once did he turn his board-stiff neck for us to even see an eyelash.

The hotel is a three story rectangle of stucco and old push-up windows with nothing to really comment on except its reasonable price. Our very little, t-shaped room on the second floor sports an iron balcony and a comforting fire escape, even though the window won't open with Herb's most vehement pushes. I think our luggage is about the same size as our room. How romantic to see the twin beds are placed foot-to-foot as if in barracks. All we expected was clean sheets and a place to sleep, so we are not disappointed in this little doll house abode. After sleeping away some of the jet lag, I decide to venture outside. A swirled floral carpet lines the hallway. Worn and outdated, it is perfect for an old English hotel. The walls leading to the glass entry are covered with an aged, drab rendition of fleur-de-lis wallpaper. I think I will write a book, "Wallpapers of the World: If They Could Speak."

It's turned into a rare sunny afternoon for London. People wear light jackets and stroll slowly with bags slung over their arms. I love to watch them, not knowing who they are, nor they me. I glimpse a sneak peak into their life. We share a common bond, people going somewhere, intent on getting to wherever "there" may be.

We have lunch at a small Chinese Restaurant near our hotel. An elderly Englishman and his family are sitting elbow-close to us—an every-word-distinguishable close. Their conversation delights me in its theatrical interplay. He apologizes for his thoughtless words, "I'm thinking with my mouth open."

We teach our children to think before they speak and warn them not to put their foot in their mouth, but never have I heard the expression, "Don't think with your mouth open."

The wife and daughter stare at him with a polite smile not of appeasement, but one that any woman would recognize. An offense of words has happened between a man and woman; the age old battle is still being fought. It gets very quiet at their table. The cold war has begun. This is turning out to be a very inexpensive vacation. We could have paid top-dollar for a play that would probably have put us to sleep, but here we are, up close and personal, to a real life drama.

A sunny Sunday morning, a perfect day for Hyde Park. Perfect, not as in flawless, but exquisite no matter what happens because we're here, we're alive and we're together. A park sign reads "Resist from chasing, worrying or harassing the animals." How could it be put more beautifully? Only a scoundrel would dream of worrying an animal. We smile at the whimsy of this quaint little sign, dwarfed by the age old trees. A blur of swan feathers glide behind their ancient black bark.

We've come upon a very large gathering of people. In fact, the next day we found out it was the largest public protest in London's history. There were over 500,000 people in a march entitled "Countryside March for Life and Livelihood" to protect the right to hunt foxes. Country people have come to London wearing hunting clothes, English plaids, and smoking pipes. They look absolutely fabulous. Three portly older Englishmen lean on an iron fence. We stop to speak to them knowing these great observers will be a good information source.

They defend what they've known as proper English form: "English don't publicly protest like this." We consider it not a protest, but a wonderful parade of people, regalia with banners flying just for us.

We visit Kensington Palace, walk through Hyde and Kensington Parks and then sit on a park bench to lunch on an apple, an energy bar and beef jerky. Just the way we like to lead our lives – walking for miles, eating outside, able to see all clearly, for doors and walls cannot hinder our view.

That evening, our choice for a restaurant is on a side street near Paddington Station. Like one of the tiny Greek isles in the Mediterranean, it is a discovery. We're thrilled with the name: Niki Taverna. It reminds me of years fleeting on the edge of a wing; they fly by quickly, almost nervously, as do our California foothill finches, coming near our country porch to feed and then flying away in a zigzagged almost indistinguishable pattern. Time has passed, birds fly, seasons change, children grow.

We remember back twenty or so years ago to our stay in Athens, a romantic island cruise, the pictures of when we were so young and less in love than we are now. The past is a shadow that follows us, the form that gives us perspective that we live today in the light.

Greek music plays. It is fun and ironic in this town dressed in formality—a wool garment to ward off cold and protect from rubbing up next to the basic human side of existence. How weather reflects a people, or shall I say, people reflect their climate.

We order lamb, vegetables and red wine. Immediately we are presented with a medley of olives and bread. The owner is present, so every worker is performing at their best. The chilly fog has wrapped itself around the trees that we see from our window.

I'm stuck on the concept of cultures tonight. I think of them as shells. Are shells for protection? Are they for beauty, yet hiding the true inward life? In maturity, are they a cumbersome coating to be cast off? Is there really an answer to these questions? Herb and I continue to ponder this as we enjoy our meal.

A man sits alone in a lump of posture over his red-checkered table cloth, talking on a cell phone so passionately I'd say it has to be his lover. His black leather jacket busily absorbs the smoke that dillies up from his half smoked cigarette. Somewhere in his sixties, his glasses are as slumped as his shoulders. They scoot down to the tip of his nose, partially camouflaging a large, ugly birthmark over his eye, a dark cloud at sunset that fades into his graying sideburns. Above him, a tarnished brass chandelier hangs precariously about two inches from an uneven hole punched in the ceiling. Two bulbs are burned out; its abdomen exposes looped intestinal wires, dressed in red tape that has lost its stickiness. I stare and wonder about the condition of the kitchen.

A mushroom-looking teen comes in to ask if the restaurant serves sandwiches. Everything is big on him, except his legs and feet. The English waitress doesn't understand his accent. He's incensed and raises his voice in triumph to say, "I'm Greek." An English waitress in a Greek restaurant in London cannot detect a Greek accent, even though the owner and his family ooze it out of not only their speech, but every gesture of their being. Irony and amusement travel with us wherever humans are to be found.

The US stock market is down to 7800, the lowest since September 11, 2001. There is pending war with Iraq's leader, Saddam Hussein, and here we are dining in London, off to Africa to love friends, build a bridge and play.

Aging lovers, bonded hearts that are woven tighter than the strongest braid, we stroll together, hand in hand, through Hyde Park—a marriage of two unique individuals at rest with each other. We kiss in this magnificent old park meant for lovers and swans under giant trees that could open a page of history for us if we could hear their voices. No taxis for us. We find our destination, Harrods, easily, and then walk back to our hotel. Six miles total.

The tube scares me even more than African snakes. Every time I walk down to its cellar basement, cold dread enters into my non-mechanical mind. I feel like I am in a commuter's riot. Frantic, fast paced English men and women are going everywhere and I don't know where everywhere is. Always feeling somewhat lost, I try not to panic. A suited man coughs on Herb. The ticket lady tells us to queue up. I ask what that means. She laughingly replies, "Take your place in line." Oh good, I thought we'd mysteriously entered an underground pool hall.

It scares me, really scares me, to try and push into the carriage before the ominous doors crush closed. I'm not comfortable. A young girl chews gum and I chew with her, without a wad in my mouth. Then she puts on lip gloss. The carriage fills to the brim. It's like most of our experiences: new, jarring, loud, sometimes dark, and full of people we don't know. These tired workday faces, worn and wrinkled from their labor, have no smiles left except for a waiting friend or family. We are pushed close to them, cramped in commuter silence, waiting for the stop where we board for our dinner cruise.

The election in Germany was reported on the news to be won by a whisker and our clerk tells us the cruise will start in two ticks. I assume by the clock, and not those little blood-sucking insects that can give Lyme disease. We take a walk to a nearby park, watching the ticks so we don't miss the cruise.

The park is well worth the tube ride experience. Its grandeur pulls me back to another century so that I imagine wearing high-topped fine kid leather boots, a summer skirt of heavy, unbleached linen with a matching fitted jacket and to top it all off, a hat with netting pulled around its wide brim so that the wind doesn't set it sailing. At one end of the park is a monument, *To the glorious and immortal memory of officers, NCOs and men of the Imperial Camel Corps, British, Australians, New Zealanders and Indians who fell in action and died of wounds and disease in Egypt, Sinai and Palestine. 1916-1918* is engraved in the marble base of the monument, atop is a bronze, life-size sculpture of a British soldier riding a saddled camel. We sit on a nearby bench so we can fully enjoy the statue and try to take in the meaning of it, if possible. Lives lost on both sides, battles fought in blistering sand, inescapable desert heat and then the last of the pain—dying in a foreign land.

The smoke from our little cigars twists upward to touch the lowest leaves of a huge sycamore tree that is lit by the park lights. I share the loss that has waned through the years, but is fresh for me tonight. We take time to wonder about this British soldier riding a camel and his many comrades.

The park is empty except for us and a homeless person, a non-gender type of survivor of our modern day. Our neighbor is toothless, but this certainly doesn't keep him or her from attempting a crossword puzzle. What strikes me most of all, amidst the unwashed clothing, is a fairly new navy knit cap that has "2002" written on it's rolled brim. A nice warm reminder of what year it is if one might forget by chance. Maybe I'll get one and wear it as others do a watch just to keep me on track. Sometimes dates and times escape me or do I push them aside on purpose? I think years, dates and titles can easily become self-important factors that can cloud us from seeing the big picture. We are so enthralled in these numbers that we forget to live the day, to experience the moment, to be thrilled by the present.

In the tiled, spotless, park loo, I mistakenly wipe myself with the back of my raincoat thinking it is tissue paper. This goes well with my aroma of cigar smoke and clothes I've worn for four days. We rarely smoke our favorite little mood cigars at home, but on vacation we find it a must for tradition sake and just plain get-away fun. Waiting for our river cruise in the chilly English night air seems to be a perfect place to join Sherlock Holmes, Winston Churchill and countless others in a smoke. I've fallen far from glamour, but Herb says "You're such a beautiful woman. All anyone has to do is look at your face and then all else doesn't matter." I've seen beauty in myself outwardly, but mostly deep in my spirit because of his consistent loving words to me over the years and lavish expressions of his untamed affection all directed toward me. Has any other woman even been so nurtured, so cherished by kindness? This is a man and a friend that I ultimately say these words about "I trust him."

Two ticks have passed, so Herb and I leave the giant sycamore park and head for the boat. I have on a blue rain jacket I bought for the rain forest in Costa Rica, a black cotton safari skirt, black walking shoes with white ankle socks that show three inches of my legs before the skirt begins, a scarf and a thermal vest. My fellow cruisers haven't walked here for sure. There is a big group of German businessmen with their wives and several Japanese couples, all tastefully dressed. I'm usually the elegant, over-dressed person, so this is a good lesson in humility.

A very pricey evening already worth every penny, for I must be in the television program, "Lifestyles of the Rich and Famous." The elegant London cityscape sparkles in the cold autumn breeze which spreads waves across the Thames as if it were a hand, moving slowly across the top of the water in a massage of ripples, relaxing tension from the water's top. A bit choppy, the water reflects the colors of the city in rainbow stripes that pierce lone stalagmites far into the deep gray where sunset or city lights cannot penetrate. I'm lost in this watery channel of surge, the ocean's mouth that pours life into the city.

After a fashionably long wait our dinner menu is presented to us. For starters, marinated artichoke, sugar snaps, pear with mixed wild salad (wild? will the lettuce strip for us or race off into the prairie on the back of a Nevada mustang?), with a cabernet sauvignon dressing.

For the main course - roast filet of salmon served with a garlic potato puree, slow roasted tomato and saffron cream sauce.

For dessert, Bailey's and white chocolate gateaux with crème anglaise and a chocolate gristine torte with a chocolate Grand Marnier sauce.

Herb says, "This is the highlight of my day and my life!" A piano bar plays "A Summer Wind." Lights low inside, the twinkle of the land lit for evening, a royal bride, a Christmas tree delight; we barely taste our meal for the passing majesty of English shore. I really like this.

The couple next to us has five minutes to show up or Herb is going to drink their champagne and eat their Greek olives. In front of us, there is a set of bongo drums draped with a hot pink feather boa. Guess there's going to be some sizzling entertainment tonight.

We cruise by the Royal Festival Hall, pass a neon blue Ferris wheel, and under a bridge we go. I'm dizzy from the moving magic of it all. Here comes Chelsea Bridge, a graceful string of lights that carry a fairytale train on its underside. The columns that hold the bridge are architecturally beautiful. Yet so solidly functional, it seems nothing could shake them. The water pushes toward us.

When we pass the next bridge, I lean backward and squint my eyes. In my mind, it turns into a silver spaceship, hovering over us in a space adventure. "Moon River" is being sung in such a sexy way I look toward the music to see the words come from the owner of the feather boa, which looks far better on her than on the bongo drums. She is a cross between Marilyn Monroe and our daughter-in-law, Cindy. She is a soft blonde, an appealing mirage that has slipped into a silver blue sateen cocktail dress which twins the sheen of the city lights that lay on the water's surface. A saxophone player to rival Kenny G accompanies her: *"Moon River, wider than a mile. I'm crossing you in style ... Moon River and me."* We approach Albert's Bridge, a two-tented strand of lights, a strand of pearls so clear only the ocean's depth could have created them, lay against the black breast of the night sky.

What seemed to be an exorbitant price a few hours ago for our river dinner cruise has become an insignificant fee for the most romantic experience Herb and I have ever had, both in complete agreement. We wed the evening as we do the past, while the band plays the Beetles' "Yesterday" and I'm nineteen again, dancing on a sawdust warehouse floor, peanut shells permissibly thrown on the floor. There's the smell of beer and sweat. My knee high leather boots crunch a shell occasionally, but I can't hear it for the sound of the sixties band belting out some free love radical, does life have any meaning, tune. I flirt with my eyes drawn to Herb across the room where I wait, sitting with my long, lean legs crossed at my thighs, and waiting for him to catch the bait. Our first dance is electric. His first time to touch me. His first time to charm me and certainly not his last. You'd think I would tire of him after all these years. For me, that idea is impossible.

Now aboard ship, we dance again. Many waters have passed since November of 1966, yet our love still grows to the honor of God, who teaches us its meaning. Handel's Messiah plays while the indoor lights are completely dimmed, so we can fully enjoy the lights of the city. Our vessel turns in a wide circle under the London Bridge as the music gives tribute to the One I hope all recognize. The words swirl in my head, *"He shall reign forever and ever, King of King and Lord of Lords..."* I put my own words to it, "creator of all things, timeless Father of all generations, ruler throughout the ages, faithful, loving God." Fantasy has come our way. A sliver of heaven has opened up for us on this starry night in a land not our own.

There is always humor in this country. The loo door on the ship says, "Engaged." Maybe the next one will say "Married," and finally the third one will say "Divorced." How do I interpret English? It takes me a while to figure things out. All the doors in the loo look the same. I push, and then pull on what seems to be an exit door, but nothing budges. A little claustrophobic, panic sets in. I breathe deeply and say to myself, "Don't panic. You're an intelligent woman. You'll be okay." All of a sudden, like the revelation one has when, falling just before you hit the ground, I realize this is not an exit door, but another occupied (or shall I say "engaged") stall. The paradigm shift happens. I'm free and safe at last to escape. Herb wonders what takes me so long. I save the exciting story for him for just the right moment, so we have time to laugh and joke about my literal, non-mechanical mind.

An evening to be relived on paper, in my dreams, and told over and over again as I snuggle close to my grandchildren on our king sized bed—an answer to their last question of the day, "Grand Mimi, tell us a story." I reserve my ticket stub memories, hoping they will pop out, unexpected, for my grandchildren as if lost in the pocket of an old, worn coat, to be found by mistake or chance. These memories, as if they were my traveling companions, will be their ticket stub to reenter the life I've lived, to hear the music of the earth we've listened to so many times. As the mist settles on the ground, just before the cold calls all to shelter in, I in defiance and compulsion stay out where there is no safety of man-made light, only sunset and dusk, calming the spirit and leading one quietly into the night.

Dreading the journey, but knowing it is inevitable, we take the tube home. My sore arm is a witness to the lesson I have learned. When the carriage door closes, it is impossible to push it open as one does an elevator door. My red and swollen wrist might was well have a sign on it that reads, "You American idiot! The rules are different here." Another foreign danger is London streets, which are the most treacherous I've attempted to cross. We've seen four people nearly hit today. Printed in big letters on the street corners are directions, either "Look to the left" or "Look to the right." Cars seem to appear from nowhere. Simultaneously, we jump back often or grab each other when there is no time for words.

Chipper, we greet a new day. We visit the Tower of London and see the Crown Jewels. Not to be missed, their loo got "Loo of the Year" award in 1995. Accolades, awards and jests of pride. I'll be curious to compare this loo with those of Kenya and then give my own award. The worst I've experienced so far is the marketplace in downtown Guadalajara, 1969. A memory I choose not to grace with words.

We walk to Regent's Park. A sign says "Park deck chairs, four-hour session for 1.50 pounds." Every nation has people selling what they can to make a living. We walk for hours past roses, park benches, and children with their school uniforms on and then lay "California-style" on the park grass for free. So many interesting people walk by, appearing as giants from our low position. Step by step, the angle from which we observe them makes it look as if they're taking huge strides forward. And we, where are we going? In our silence, we are resting from the day and preparing emotionally to take the leap. It is a flight of faith for Herb and I, as two slender arrows propelled by fate and desire across the sea, over nations and into the Dark Continent.

I look to Herb, the man I've loved since my teens, hated several times over, but somehow always adored. I ask myself, "Who did this to you? You're older now, a reminder that all is passing and will be no more." Our lives are as bright as a noonday cloud, soon to be swept away by the invisible wind as if they had never been. How did what existed pass by so quickly? Not a morbid, hopeless thought, but one that brings me nothing but balance and thankfulness. I look to Herb. I see a blanket of silver hair woven with gray in Navajo style, still a dark brown strand here and there to remind me of the days of his dark, curly youth. A "touch me" thick crop of hair pulled back in a tail as if a pirate was in my presence. Years have grown and pulled his eyebrows into an upward snow drift that form arching curves over his determined brown eyes. I am convinced these eyes represent, in equal proportion, given to him by God, a deep, dark resolve that haunts him day or night. He is driven by passion and concern for others. Handsomely weathered, worn to show his character, for one must ask, "I wonder what kind of life that man has lived?" A tattered well-read book that invites others to pick it up, a supple spirit, pressed and torn by life, he is my husband. He is the one who breathes on me.

The passersby have lost their charm. I am again daydreaming about the father of my children, now a grandfather, a man of moral fiber, my mate for life.

We walk to our hotel. It begins to rain. This is appropriate as everything is now a mundane blur, a ritual to perform until we are at last on the plane for Nairobi.

PART II: KENYA AT LAST

We take a night flight and sleep in a scrunch until morning wakes us (or is it the pain that radiates up my back, into my crooked neck?) I feel restless and bare as our plane makes its approach. I've been warned to leave my wedding ring in California. I do wear a three carat tiger's eye set high in a wide silver band. If they cut my finger off for it, so be it.

I'm not sure what to expect at the Nairobi airport. I hope we get our luggage without it being opened and all my valuables stolen, such as hiking shoes, hiking shorts and my favorite sun hat. The rest seems unimportant. Waiting with a smile that has the power to change your mind about almost anything is our charismatic, not-to-be-put-in-a-box friend. He is the unlikely missionary breaking all the stereotypes of those who go to serve Christ in foreign places. Harmon Parker, the only Harmon I've ever met, is as uncommon as his name. Lean and fit, he is ready for whatever adventure or unexpected peril awaits him. He is ready and waiting for us—an undertaking at which many might cower. Harmon is a gentle, passionate man, who is unarmed except for his surprising great humor, a tool that disarms the threat of danger. From the moment his smile reaches across the room to shake us into security, until we leave six weeks later, Harmon and his wife, Teri, are the consummate caregivers.

Years later, we meet a woman on a Sierra trail. She sees Herb's hiking stick carved with the names of places we hiked in Africa. She lived in Somalia and said, "Africa is a place where you need to have someone who knows how to keep you safe." How concise and true her statement was! If I hadn't been to Kenya and Tanzania, her words would have fallen underfoot just as the autumn leaves that fell onto the trail to be disregarded and crushed into the dirt path.

All is loaded into Harmon's Land Rover: suitcases and our wary traveler's bodies hyped with excitement and the laughter that follows us everywhere. We are filled with nervous expectation and are submerged in a watery joy, so fluid I am drenched in it. The Land Rover is full. All I can think is, "This is fun. We may die, but so what. This is so fun."

Nairobi is the only airport in the world to have a game park next to its runway. The airport building is quite adequate, but I am fully aware we are in a third world country. After weeks here, I call it a fourth world country. It's early morning, the day is so bright. I adjust to its glare but it doesn't deter me from seeing a new country. I smell calm in the air mixed with heat and the scent of people, a mixture of nationalities that all seem dull compared to the gorgeous jet black skin of Kenyans. They are arrows darting by—dark sculptured masterpieces—the people I came to be with. My heart is racing, hungry for the adventure of learning. I salivate to see more, to know this land, to at last walk the earth of Kenya.

Our drive to Harmon's house instantly ignites all my senses, as if they were a stacked pyre of kindling waiting for a magic match. Africans lounge everywhere on the ground. Some sleep, others talk with friends, stretched out vulnerably on their stomachs with heads lifted to make eye contact. Others are sprawled under trees to rest from the ever-present sun. They resemble giant blossoms, freshly fallen from the mighty limbs, inseparable from each other. The bed of earth from which they seem to have grown is their friend. The ground, hard and cracked, welcomes them to be a part of it, as if it were some distant relative yearning for the contact of their skin, to hear the story of their lives, to be told when their weary bodies lay on it in a dead-weight exhaustion. I see dark bodies wrapped, tied and intricately knotted in print fabrics, living angular pillows tossed casually on the velvet brown couch of earth. Here or there is a smiling face that draws me so intensely that I want to walk into its mystery and stay. Elbows and legs, such bony sticks, hold up their living tents with so much beauty in their graceful movements. They have a rhythm, a gait seen with the eye that is willing to join in with glee and an appreciation as vast as the country itself.

Our Land Rover passes people living out their everyday lives in a great theatrical performance, pushing primitive carts, carrying immense burdens of all types on their heads, walking miles to accomplish the simplest daily chores. The privilege of being a part of this is a bit more, a far bit more than I can take in. What they must think of me with my white face sailing by, hair blowing in the welcome breeze, blue eyes opened wide with my jaw dropped in astonishment. What a sight for them! I whisk by in another world, propelled by machinery. Harmon avoids dangerous neighborhoods to hopefully ensure our safety.

Really now, is there anywhere in the world where we are safe? In California, I buckle my seatbelt and drive the freeways, usually above the posted speed limit, always keeping up, keeping up with the pace of traffic, the pace of life. I hike the mountains with a partner or my trusted bear spray. I lock my doors, set the house alarm and wonder if it will be violence or the silent hand of disease that will reach in to claim my life? I do what I can to not worry and agree with others that life is uncertain, yet not so uncertain in Saratoga, California, which is one of the safest and wealthiest communities in the world. Am I safe there or here in Kenya? It's the honesty of Africa that I feel safe in. One knows beyond doubt that it is not safe here, and then lives life to the fullest, shaking hands with the inevitable to settle the issue that our stay on earth is truly brief.

California has so much to offer that one develops discrimination between fine lines of fun and more fun. Opportunity and opulence, the twins that surround our normal existence begin to shrink in the early morning African sun. Kenya, a place of beauty and stabbing poverty, can rob even the most hopeful of their youthful vision. Still, the zest for life, an insurmountable spirit, reigns above the ruins. We pass the beginning of the Kiberia slums, a dirt pathway that runs for miles, where over seven hundred thousand people live in abject poverty. There is no running water, electricity, toilets or garbage pickup, only mountains of waste that separate less than shacks from the waste their bodies have discarded. Years of death, disease and heartache have built these walls of hopeless filth. The stench passes by quickly for we have our windows rolled up, doors locked and air conditioning on. Harmon, whom I've named, "the kind man," mentions their plight with a compassion that drew him and his wife, Teri to this country over fifteen years ago to serve the people. We head to Nairobi's heart and then on to where Harmon and Teri live. The traffic has come to a very slow roll. Who knows why? The men guess maybe an accident. Only five minutes pass and we see a policeman directing traffic on the right side of the road. Harmon says, "Don't look. Someone is dead."

At first I see a bicycle folded in half, bars turned toward the new day in a cry for help. My heart jumps as if I might be able to help somehow. My eyes blink and there in the dirt byway is a twisted man, his knees pointing toward the city, while his feet bent backwards and lead to nowhere. His mouth, pouring out the last of life's blood is open to the exhaust of commuters who barely turn their eyes to look. I took him in as an act of respect. He wasn't a discarded, crumpled napkin of inconvenience to litter the highway. He wasn't another tally of death along with the birth count of the day. He was a brother on his bike, doing his best to survive, but not given the dignity of an old sheet to cover his distorted face. Most people sleep without sheets, why waste one on the dead?

Once again we are in the reality of a third world country, the reality of life. In a prayer, Herb pours out sympathy and help for the dead man's family. We silently agree with his words. Earlier that morning, if I had seen the man, I would have called him the man on the bicycle, pedaling hard, headed off for the day. Now I call him the dead man. Night has fallen and it is only morning. There was no lingering bedside vigil, no gradual loss that helps to introduce one to the inevitable, only a sudden volt, and a lightening strike of fate or chance. There is something Old Testament about his body sprawled so awkwardly on the red earth. "By the sweat of your brow you will eat your food until you return to the ground, since from it you were taken; for dust you are and to dust you will return" (Genesis 3:19.)

We pass a man redirecting his empty cart, street-side flower stands to rival the color and beauty of the fabled San Francisco French flower carts, and people walking, people that seem much taller than they actually are because their heads are held high above their whisper of a body. They come in a constant stream, pouring out of the slums as if the earth, like an immense pitcher, is held spout downward in a never-ending flow of people. They're on their way to work or the daily search for work. They all seem related, not by blood, but by the bond of survival. The grip of poverty is so strong it has the lock-jar hold of a pit bull in a fight to the end. I have nothing but admiration for the people who walk so majestically. Conquerors of each day, there must be royalty in their blood.

Harmon and Teri's compound is less than an hour drive from the airport, in the Gigiri District of Nairobi, situated next to the Swedish Ambassador's home. Albert, Harmon's yard man and day watchman, greets us at the tall iron entry gate with a smile that is so sincere, I feel we must be a part of him and are now aware that he is our long lost brother. Is Albert a message, often missed, of what heaven will be like when the gates are opened for us? The spirit of a man shines through his eyes and I recognize of course, my kin, my brother in Christ.

The three guard dogs circle our Land Rover, barking an indistinguishable biting sound into the moist air, threatening or yelling out canine pleasure to see us. I am unable to determine which. We slowly proceed up the steep, flower-bordered driveway with the cheers of the dogs making it evident that a celebration is ours. All is well! The rattle over cobblestone stops and we are here, in front of the Parker's home. Adventure awaits us as does everyday we have eyes to perceive what our hearts are willing to open up to. I see an old, one-story structure with white iron bars that have tops shaped like spears, which form a protective encampment around the front entrance. It reminds me of Fiji or Aruba or some tropical island far from home, where we have visited in the past. It's luxurious, yet primitive, a home of warmth, gracious Christian hospitality, a place where all life is honored. We slip off our shoes in the entryway to feel the cool tile absorb the heat from our bodies. Camel-toned walls pull us into a haven where I expect to see the Savior's shadow in the quiet hallway. This is where I want to be and where I will contentedly stay for such a short season.

Teri, all that a parent would want in a daughter, is the essence of this home. A foreigner in an unknown land, she thrives. We feed on her beauty and think how brave she was to move to Kitale, near the west Pokot, with her husband and three-year old son, Joshua. She had no resources but her faith. So brave and daring, she would enter hand-in-hand with Daniel into the den, lions waiting. It's been years since their primitive home in Kitale, where ravenous dogs roamed the night. Now in the huge city of Nairobi, other perils are ever present.

We've come as Kenya's spring has just started. The warm weather must be an optimistic sign of what is before us. The drenching rains and mud are gone.

Out cottage is an out-building to the right side of the main house. We walk through the kitchen, a haven in itself and pass under the veranda that leads onto an open patio. Around the house and down the walkway is our humble abode that has a heavy wooden door. The best surprise awaits us as we open what I call "the door of delights." Our expectations are still sleeping or somewhere floating in jet lag. What charm! Everything says "we've been waiting for you, can hardly stand it 'til you're here!" A bouquet of two dozen roses, fruit bowl, and chocolates sit on the crude wooden table. On a shelf are imported teas, juice and (calming my fears) a big jug of purified water. The main room has a dinner table, a kitchen sink and to the side, a toilet and an old shower. It's one that I look at with disdain and snobbery and at the same time, great thankfulness to have running water. The shower represents to me the contrast between life in Kenya and life in Saratoga. It's all in perspective. What is a bathroom for but to bathe? Why does one need space for three bodies in a cubicle that 99% of the time houses one? Why does one need Italian marble or the finest Spanish tile to surround us, when we're scrubbing off the day's sweat and dirt? It washes down the drain and off we go, all human beings, scrubbed clean for the next task that besets us. When do status, value and self-worth lie in the size of our bathrooms? Certainly not here in the Gigiri District. It lays at the feet of Jesus in humility, honoring others, and respecting their personhood.

How secure I feel tucked away in this little cottage, zebra rug underfoot, darkness falling ever so quickly. It is evening of our first day. We dine on the veranda, admiring the hillside of colorful flowers dwarfed by neighboring trees. The table is dressed in a blue tie-dyed cloth, orange roses and bird of paradise as the centerpiece. The wicks of the candles stand perfectly upright, for there is not a breath of wind, barring the laughter and deep sighs of enjoyment to hear each other's stories. These stories span the breadth of life or describe the humor seen in the common day. They are told by those who love each other, so they all have our attention. They rate significance because the lips who utter them are significant.

Some call this fellowship, some friendship. I call this truly living life. The light of day is gone, so near the equator. We barely see each other but for the candlelight. Here in the shadows, we hear and taste the person. Façades aside, we are together.

Teri prepares Chai, a very strong tea, for the night watchman. He stays up all night to guard the compound. I think of him as my own secret service man and am thankful he is watching out for us as we sleep. Stretched out atop my covers, I recall the day. It's been ointment to my soul. I try reluctantly to let go of it. Ironically, sleep seems to be an enemy instead of my treasured friend. My thoughts of pleasure slowly fade into the night air through the iron bars of our bedroom window, flying high into the sky. I watch them go in a smile of contentment as if I've released a balloon of joy for it to go where the winds may take it. Dogs bark in the distance. Our first day in Kenya is over only because of time restraints, never in my memory. Even when I'm so old I forget all else, today will be embedded so deep within my spirit that only death will part it from me.

The beds were wonderfully comfortable but I wake with a sore back from the flight. Harmon says he has the perfect remedy for me—a massage. I willingly surrender to the decadence and off we go to the health club. The young Kenyan woman, a sweet sparkle in her eye, seemed to have equal pleasure in serving me as I do being treated with such kindness. She presses and rubs away the soreness of my muscles. I am a lump of dough lying on the table. I love paying her. We smile big at each other like little girls playing house. It was her part to give me the massage, mine to give her the money. I hope it helps her survive in this harsh, impoverished country. I'd like to spend a day with her, twenty-four hours in her world. I can only imagine. It would probably shock me to equal proportion as it would her to slip into my skin, go out to greet Harmon and Herb as Lynn and live my life for one day. My wish is that she is as spoiled with love and affection in her family as I am with Herb.

The men greet me in the lobby with a question that I could tell Harmon couldn't wait to get out of his mouth,"How was it?" His childlike grin pushes up his cheeks to meet fine lines that have formed under the corners of his eyes from years of laughter. It seems they vicariously enjoyed me getting a massage as much as I did getting one. I laughed as we walked into the Kenyan sun, which joined us as if it were another member of our party. My laughter was the answer to their question. We all know it, but a woman who sees pictures painted with words has to answer in words. Frail as they were in properly supporting the essence of what I was feeling I went ahead: "It feels like I'm floating face upwards under a foot of clear water, hidden, yet fully exposed. She started with my heels, my feet and then worked upwards pressing hard into my muscles and then gently slapping my flesh in a rhythmic wave, I her willing drum. Kenya has begun its magical relaxing hold on me. I give myself to her and all that God is willing to show me during our brief stay."

Teri takes Herb and I to Aughiti Indian restaurant. Under their name is written "The Masters of Indian Cuisine." We have mutton Kashmiri (lamb), palace pander (spinach), dal makani (black beans) and Madras (chicken.) We all proclaim the meal to be excellent and their sign accurate. They've tamed the culinary experience artfully, like a tiger trainer who is in full control of the powerful beast. No spice too hot, the flavors entertainingly delicious. We are full and captivated by each course, delighted by the Indian owner and our server.

Teri drives by a nursery on our way home and Herb, the gardener that he is, asks for her to stop. There is a young African woman with a baby slung on her held by a long piece of printed fabric. She is watering potted plants that have been placed under the giant trees that grow up the steep mountainside. Teri says at night, people with dangerous intentions come out of this forest and down near the street and that driving at night is very risky. Theft and car-jackings are common. Teri asks the woman's permission for us to take her picture. She seems surprised and agrees. We pay her 100 shillings (US $1.25) which is near the amount of her day's wages. Teri said it will help feed her family or buy milk for her baby. I want to paint or sculpt the beautiful black garden woman with her heavy tin watering can.

It's Friday and Teri wants to take us to the neighborhood open-air market that is crowded with merchants who come to sell their goods. She knows we'll love it and she is right! The sun is intense. I feel it pushing through my hat and clothing to scorch my skin. I look for shade but there is little to be found, only under the eaves of the permanent shops. Teri turns to me and says with astonishment, "They, the merchants, stand in the sun all day long. It is sweltering and they are smiling." I buy African jewelry, of course, and Teri helps me by haggling with her long developed skill of monetary diplomacy (the art of conducting fair settlements) and helps me make change. Without my own personal shopper I'd be paying four times the going price for my goods. After years in Kenya, Teri knows when to laugh, when to joke and when to cut to the core. The sellers are happy with a fair price and smile a quirky respectful twist of their mouths as if it were a hidden signal, a mystery wink to let her know they'd enjoyed the exchange.

Kenyan music is playing, and people are pushing in and out, around each other as if to weave an invisible tapestry of the day. Armed guards are posted everywhere in the marketplace, even in the parking lot to watch the cars. It's exciting, foreign, and so loud with life and sound that I keep thinking, "Can someone please turn down the volume a bit, or at least slow down the motion?" I can't take it all in at this pace. There is no answer to my unspoken question. So I try to adjust to the frenzy, unwind and enjoy instead of retreating into my staid western culture. It's all a matter of letting go.

As I choose to relax I start to see it. This is a party! Kenyans living in the moment; tomorrow is not even a consideration. Today, now, is the festival of life as if they've peeked into heaven and see what joy really looks like. They are my teachers, my example—they are my holiday. It's all been a skillful game the sellers and buyers have developed over eons of time. Teri is my younger sister, wise in her element, knowing how to play the game and to protect me. All are happy.

I follow her lead and come out with a very fair price for amber, silver and bone jewelry, all ethnic to the core. Around us is a sea of wood carvings, baskets, fabrics, beaded and tooled belts, woven hand bags, carved gourds, people, laughter, sweat and heat! I have new African jewelry, a cloth kikoi, a woven sisal purse, but most of all, I have treasures to remember my day shopping under the searing open sky, no mall or roof for comfort, and undergarments sticking to my body as if I'd had an hour long menopausal hot flash.

The Parker's rented home is only a long dirt-and-broken-asphalt street away from the marketplace so we arrive home in about the time it takes to fasten and unfasten our seatbelts. In that short time, Teri has ample time to be a defensive driver. We joke about how one obtains a driver's license here. It may be through family influence or a bribe under the table. Whatever it is, we are maneuvering on the wild side. All I can do is laugh. Herb takes it a bit more seriously, always the protector.

Once at home again, Harmon greets us with his warm smile that convinces me he's been waiting patiently for us all afternoon. We follow his lead to the outdoor porch enclosed by a wall of cinderblock, candles are placed here and there in-between the wall's open spaces. They have formed an artful waterfall of wax on the wall, indicating many evenings have been spent here in the sweet light of candles, memories of the day shared, closure subtle and beautiful, still and warm as a sunset taken in at the end of the day's light.

We're enclosed on three sides by plants, a couch and two chairs, padded by colorful soft pillows, and throws if the night air turns chilly. We smile and laugh at almost anything, the way friends do. We recall the day and try in a calm desperation to fill in the hollow spaces of life since we've been together. Time holds still. I read my poetry.

Harmon sings while he plays his guitar. Teri listens with her heart and Herb shakes his head hard enough that his pony tail flips from one side to the other, and says, "Life is too good at this moment." There is harmony. The Parkers call this "porch time." I think this is a bit of heaven on earth. Dinner is about to be served, but who wants to eat? We have been fed on the richest life has to offer. Moments like this are lasting. Trouble just like the seasons will return in it's time and we all know without the exchange of words, that being together somehow fulfills our destiny.

After dinner, Herb and I walk around the main house to our little cottage. Teri comes over to let us know that the night guard hasn't shown up. This is not a good sign. She instructs us what to do if there is a break-in. The guard could have been paid off, a very real possibility in Nairobi. We lay as easy prey without a guard to stay up all night protecting the compound. She tells us to lock our cottage door and then lock ourselves into the bedroom. The heavy wooden door, castle-like in its thickness, will hopefully shut out harm when Herb turns the big, old fashioned key to the right with a strong twist of his wrist. I feel like I'm living out the third chapter of a Sherlock Holmes mystery. Suspense mixed with reality sends a sober chill up my spine. The two guard dogs are on duty. Mr. Big, the Jack Russell Terrier, is inside the main house. Our instructions are to hide under the bed or face our bodies toward the wall if intruders break in and to never look at their face or they will kill us. As long as we can't identify them, we don't have to worry about losing our lives. Rape is not an issue as they are after money and valuables. The Swedish ambassador's compound is directly behind the Parker's back yard. They have two night guards with a trained attack dog that patrol their grounds all night. It's the other three sides of the property that present a challenge. Teri reminds us that she has two panic buttons installed in the main house. If one is pushed, a vehicle with five men comes within minutes. They are a ferocious rag-tag army with motorcycle helmets on, shields held high, and clubs. If the front gate is locked, they scale over it. Teri has tested the panic button and says the experience is a frightening show. I hope I will not be witnessing this Kenyan SWAT team tonight.

Herb and I get into our twin beds. They are close enough for us to hold hands while we pray. I'm not afraid, only thankful to be a part of this great adventure. Tonight the fear of harm holds no grip on me. We sleep well until barking dogs wake us at four in the morning. I peek thought the iron bars of our only small window to see that the darkness has lifted enough to make out the form of trees that stagger in height so high I cannot see their tops. I shrink back into my bed and think of a poem I wrote and then fall back to sleep...

One event leads into another
Steps made toward the future,
Our destiny uncovered.
Let's travel on a journey of
Mysterious time.
Moving forward, in constant
Motion our destiny untwines.
Some march, others twist into
A fearful coil.
In the ever present effort,
Onward movement, our enemy
Of stagnation is failed.
Heads held high, future hope,
We are looking to the coming day.
Trust in our Savior, our guide
Now and always.

Teri has prepared a delicious, huge breakfast to send Harmon, Herb and I off to build the bridge in the west Pokot. The first leg of the trip is about a six hour drive north. Harmon has packed the Land Rover and trailer with all we will need. Teri makes sure we have enough water and sanitary hand wipes. I don't use hand wipes at home, so this is a new concept for me. She says people will want to shake our hands, especially the children and to be sure to use the wipes. Disease runs rampant in the west Pokot, one of the most primitive places in the world. I use the wipes but never in sight of the people whom I wouldn't want to insult.

After all is settled for the drive, I go back into the house. Everyone is outside, except Roselyn, Teri's helper. The job Harmon and Teri have provided for her has made it possible for Roselyn to care for her four children after her husband left her with nothing. She is standing in the kitchen wearing a black and white traditional maid uniform, which she insists on wearing. I guess it must be a badge of honor for her, but for me it's like a psychedelic flashback to the fifties. I guess her to be 5' 4" tall, round and strong. Her face and feet are my favorite parts of her body. Her hair cropped about an inch long, forms a tight curly cap to frame her shiny black skin. Eyes, large dark pebbles, quick to show expression, compete in beauty with her wide, open, unafraid smile. Her extremely calloused feet are bare and flat like a platypus. They've gone naked for years, so there is only a slight raised area where the arch should be. The tops are tuxedo dark in contrast to the fleshy pink soles. She immediately smiles at me and I take the initial step toward her with arms open. We laugh a love laugh, as I embrace my sweet sister on equal footing. One woman, one mother, one person bonded together by Christ's love that spans color, age and culture. Respect flows back and forth through our embrace. Life so unpredictable here, she gives me a love farewell as if it will be her last opportunity. A vulnerable servant, her knowledge of the world so limited, yet her wisdom of life runs as deep as a high mountain river. She understands how life can change direction forever as quickly as a turn of the head. Softly her words come out of a tender smile, "I will pray for you. Christ is everything to me." She pauses, looks straight into my eyes as someone does just before they hand you a gift and describes her faith in the Messiah in the most meaningful way I have ever heard, "Without Him, without Him, I could not breathe." I am so stunned that all I can do is kiss her for sharing in such an intimate way with me. How I admire her and imagine her seated in heaven, rows ahead of me. I've been with someone of importance.

All things fit smoothly together and I realize that Roselyn is my beginning to an incredible drive and then entry into the west Pokot. I'm coming more and more to the conclusion that Christ still walks the earth not in the form of Jesus' body, but that He is revealed through hearts that have been conformed to Him. I leave Roselyn but take with me a purifying fragrance of humility, a lasting incense I still breathe in.

Going somewhere unknown makes me want to hold onto the past for security, even grab the side of our Land Rover for stability. My Jaguar at home makes me sink into its luxurious comfort. No death grip for me in my daily, familiar drive to the store, friends' houses or shopping malls. All is calm and well in my affluent life of comfort, driving wherever my heart wishes. Here I keep asking myself, "What's that noise? Why is it so bumpy? Where's the air conditioner? Where in the world am I anyway?"

I must be back in my mom's 1950 Ford, tumbling over a crude dirt road on a Saturday Ozark morning, delivering our garbage out to the county dumps. My two siblings and I were allowed the treat of riding on the hood of the car. We'd hold on to each other and the two lucky center passengers would grab the hood ornament. Up and down the rolling, dusty road, our hair flying, bugs galore, wet with humidity by nine in the morning. It was a time before seat belts were ever thought of and mom, free spirit as she is, could throw caution to the wind in an instant if it meant giving us a thrill. She took us to our own imaginary theme park, poor as we were; my single mom raising three kids gave us a roller coaster ride. Rules and restrictions flew out the windows and landed in some gnarly Missouri half-dried bush. Off I go some fifty years later, a heart wild and free, on a childlike adventure. I am very young again, even though I'm grown.

We are "off for the races," a term my Midwestern relatives taught me, and up we go through the winding streets of Nairobi to higher country where the tea and flower farms thrive in the fertile red earth. It's Sunday so people dressed in their very best are walking alongside the highway to church, heat not a deterrent. I'd be wet and suffering from hairspray failed, blisters on my feet and a very bad attitude once I arrived at the sanctuary if I attempted to do what they do. Yes, the church would truly feel like a sanctuary after the five-mile trek. We have friends who live east of Nairobi who report that some of their parishioners walk up to ten miles one way to get to church. To Kenyans, this is a normal, small cost to pay to achieve their goal of worshiping with fellow believers. Worship is an all day affair.

I'm afraid for the people. We're on the main freeway of the country, which is a two-lane pothole road with no center-divide, few guard rails and no safe place to pull to the side. Most of the time, we travel at sixty to sixty-five miles per hour. Many pass us going much faster. Next to the road's edge, close enough for me to lean out and touch, are people walking, small children playing, and goats, cows and chickens running free. I ask Harmon, "What would happen if someone hit a child?" He says a mob would come out and stone you if you waited around, so he'd pick up the child and drive to the nearest hospital. I'm shocked by his answer and sit in silence. I need to think about it for a while, just as it took me a while to soak in the newspaper article about a woman being killed because she was suspected of being a witch.

I pensively turn to see the sun reflecting off the high, slick foreheads of dark-faced people wearing jewel-toned garments so brilliant in color they seem to move on their own, apart from their owners. A tall man wearing a turquoise shirt walks slowly through a corn field, children hang on each other, and a donkey cart wobbles side to side, obese with a high stack of sheep skins. A little boy who looks less than ten years old whips his donkey to gain a faster pace. I cannot detect even a grimace on the donkey's face as the whip slashes back and forth across his hide. I see cruelty. Others may see nothing but the normal way to get your animal going.

The higher we climb, the more life around me and in me changes. We're now at 8,000 feet, where pine trees imported by the Brits thrive. I've lost the word for boredom. It has no meaning here. I think the process began somewhere in my imagination of Africa on the flight, or maybe in my dreams of coming to a place that causes my heart to race in fearful excitement of the unknown. Wherever it began, boredom fled quietly, here and then gone, like a bothersome gnat that distracts one from the joy of the journey and then disappears. I'm certainly not going to look for it. In fact, the whole concept of boredom escapes me, for even now as I write, the country of Kenya entertains me with her lasting pictures, a cinema of pleasure. A scene of simple hard life, a farmer's plight, the struggle of the poor to survive and the joy of contentment in their work is all around me. They are people who live in community. Here is a village, a tribe, a small town of ingenious people rising high above the earth's harsh elements, disease and the ever-present threat of wild animals. They are uncomplicated victors that, by example, shame us for our whining about so-called hardships in the Land of Plenty.

We stop at the Hotel Kunste, in the town of Nakuru, for lunch. The hotel must have been quite fashionable in its day. There are huge jacaranda trees overburdened with purple blossoms and birds I don't recognize flying and singing as if they are here to introduce us to the first act of a marvelous play. The sweet yet strong fragrance of plumeria makes paradise come true, for if I smell it then it must be real. Its five-petaled pink blossom looks like a star. If I designed a flag for our trip to build Kathryn's Crossing, it would have a large plumeria in the center with birds flying upward across the petals. So much like Kathryn—feminine, a life that draws you in to her freely, a spirit that reaches high above her circumstances. Kathryn, with her southern charm, would fit here perfectly.

We enter the hotel veranda, the garden posted like centurions on either side of us. There's something regal, wedding-like in this grand old entrance. We sit in the open air with a view of the garden. It is so still, that not even a leaf moves from the lacy tree in front of us. The worn rattan furniture squeaks painfully, as I adjust to what seems to be an African Great Gatsby scene. Harmon says, "Order anything. It's safe." This tickles me, as if Harmon would ever bring us to place where he knew the food was unsafe. Yes, in this area of the world, I'm sure he's learned to reassure many a visitor. The heat is rising off the wet grass. I order a safe Coke and two hard-boiled eggs. It does seem a little dangerous to me when I see where the chickens live. I put it out of my mind as I do the thought of meat processing plants in the United States. The men order a chicken sandwich. The table is quiet except for my racing mind trying not to miss a sound or movement. A white-breasted raven flies overhead to the rhythm of workers speaking Swahili. I stare at a candelabra-armed cactus long enough to realize my cousin Kathryn's presence is especially strong.

I am quite aware of her sweet love like a calming balm that makes life's intolerable moments, tolerable. How happy she must be in heaven. It's as if she's sharing some of her joy with me in equal proportions to the pain I saw her graciously live through in her fight against colon cancer. Who would have said that she, a seemingly healthy wife, mother, daughter and friend to so many would die so young, at forty-two years old.

It was the beginning of the year that she began to feel ill. Several months passed to come up with a correct diagnosis and then the struggle for life began. I had the privilege of flying to Mesquite, Texas to be with her and my Aunt Betty, near the end of her life, or shall I say her "crossing."

As she lived, she died. She had the same faith-filled determination, a resolve to love Jesus and others even as she slipped into a coma and passed from this life. We sang her into heaven with one of her favorite hymns, her last breath a gentle sigh and then the summer rains began. So final, she left her body. So eternal, she is alive forever. The bridge's name was something Herb and I poured thought into since planning our trip to Kenya. In Kathryn's hospital room, it came to me as clearly as the call of the African Go Away bird; Kathryn's Crossing.

Our meal is finished and there is still a long drive ahead. My secret is dear. I've been with Herb and Harmon, the two most charming men I've ever known, on the great veranda. But I have truly been with Kathryn. Her memories leave a satisfying taste in my mouth as we leave our table.

When I think of Kathryn I can't help but think of her mother, my Aunt Betty. If only every person on this earth had an Aunt Betty, what an ideal place this world would be. Betty, a woman who exudes love and acceptance from her every pore is my model. I stand close to her to watch and listen, hoping that some of her character will rub off on me. Since I was a child, she has made me feel safe and special. Many childhood memories end in adult reality and disillusionment, but not so with my Aunt Betty. All that is remembered is the same. She is a quiet fortress, a sweet strength I can lean on.

Betty has experienced multiple losses, hardship and has turned to Christ for her example of how to suffer, endure and come out purified as a result.

Betty's first daughter was born without an esophagus. After two years in and out of the hospital and many operations, she died. Twelve years passed without another child and at last, healthy baby Kathryn was born. Then came my Uncle Ross' prolonged illness and his parting. All the while, Betty was the bread-winner of the family while having my stroke-impaired grandmother live with her. Now her only remaining child is about to leave this world. How she can even stand up alone amazes me! She is a queen, an overflowing spring of patience, humility and faith. She will always be next to perfect to me, but oh how I shy away from the process that has refined her. She has climbed the mountain slowly, always persevering as her eyes are fixed on the hope that lives within her. A woman who laughs with a youthful giggle, loves to feed and comfort others, she has reached the pinnacle of insight. My Aunt Betty is a self-fulfilled, accomplished woman who is selfless. She is the example of all I strive to become.

The coolness of the shade ceases when I start the short walk toward the car. I reach for my sun hat but realize it will only be seconds until I am in the car.

Harmon checks the supplies for the bridge that are in the trailer we pull behind us. Still a very long, bumpy drive until we reach Kitale, the town I imagine waits for us. Off we go onto the African trans-highway, where each village sports a hello with their most flourishing crop stacked by the roadside, in hope of a sale. It may be potatoes, carrots, beets or whatever the elevation or soil deems best. Harmon slows as we approach a town. The people run to our car as fast as a starving person would toward a meal. There is a mass of people, merchant farmers, engulfing the car with pleas of us to buy, a few smiles and aggressive pushes against our locked doors. Our windows are rolled down enough for breathing room. I am invigorated by the color of their produce, the passion of their persuasive shouting in Swahili for us to buy and terrified if I let myself as their pleas take on a violent tone. Merchants are jabbing long bunches of dirty carrots into the windows, demanding that we purchase them. It feels like a mob scene. It looks like a mob climbing on the hood of the car, so thick I cannot see sunlight through them. How will my family receive the news that we were killed in a struggle over carrots? Knowing the way I love carrots will take some of the pain away, I'm sure. I say, "We've been accosted by the carrot people."

Laughing so hard we can hardly find where we have hidden our money, we purchase some produce and head out of the frenzy. We've been infused by the experience and for the next hour create a glowing orange fable about the Land of the Carrot People. A place where carrots grow inches longer each day, where the people only wear orange, have perfect sight and all wear six carat diamond rings for their labors. Carrot muffins are served for breakfast, carrot coleslaw for lunch, carrot soup for dinner, sautéed carrots and a bit of honey carrot for dessert. On and on, the fable of the red-headed carrot people goes until we laugh so hard that my only goal is to find a toilet. It's been the kind of game that parents wish their children would play on long road trips to pass the time. It's the type of fun one has when being childlike and vulnerability is admired by friends.

We speed down the treacherously curved road. I linger over thoughts of the carrot people. I wish we could have bought every carrot they owned, leaving them a big tip with our car slowly driving off and their hands full of bills, waving at us as if they had just won the lottery. Our car would be full to the brim with carrots rubbing against our pale skin until we turned orange with happiness and their lives the better for our purchase. I fantasize a better life for people whose only existence is to get others to buy their carrots by the wayside.

This country is so delightful and so terribly harsh. There are thirty million people living in Kenya. At this point, seven hundred die each day of AIDS, mostly without medicine or proper medical care. Little groups of children, from four to five to thirty, cluster together, parenting each other. This tenderness must come directly from the heart of God.

Female circumcision is still practiced or, "performed" as I prefer to say. I like to reserve the word "practice" for medicine, not butchery. This procedure is done with a crude knife, no anesthetic, no sterile environment, only the goal of cutting off a young girl's clitoris, her pleasure center. Harmon took a picture of such a girl. It is in his office and a daily reminder of the culture to which he ministers. I can recall her face in a moment. It is painted white, her eyes a bloodshot stare of agony. I suffer with her and then turn my thoughts away so as not to fall into a hopeless pit of questions that seem unanswerable. Without female circumcision, a man will not marry a woman, and she most likely will never have children—a sentence equaling a daily emotional death for an African woman. They are deformed, develop horrific infections and sometimes die.

PART III: AN ADVENTURE IN WEST POKOT

West Pokot, remote and poorer than dirt, is a place where very little and a smoke-filled dark hut used for shelter are two essentials for survival. Such luxuries as toilet paper, Band Aids, Q-tips, sanitary napkins, hand cream, soap, and toothbrushes are non-existent. Life is bare—bare-naked to the bone from what I know. They are without!

Sorrow and beauty mingle together in a dance I have never seen before, sometimes excruciatingly slow and sometimes wildly primitive, calling one to join in the celebration of life and into the struggle for sheer existence. I can hear the song playing in my heart, echoing in its chambers while I still my soul, long enough to listen. Its lyrics speak of life being hard, sorrow running deep and God being good. In it, there is a call to be authentic, to search for my Creator's hand in all I see, and alas! A search for freedom—freedom to accept the imperfections I see in myself and others.

If we were stripped of our electricity—oh no, God forbid no television, cars, computers radios, etc!—IF we were just us, without the robbing other, what might we see? What might we hear if we let ourselves be freed from our modern conveniences? If the rising sun or the sound of birds woke us, if the setting sun signaled we only had a glimmer left of twilight and then it was time to build a fire, if we walked everywhere we went, what would we become? Does convenience and technology rule our lives?

I dream of living this way for one year. Would living unencumbered, help me answer these questions, or would my life become the answer? What do I truly value? To where has the art of listening from the heart disappeared? How much a part of my life is filled with hopeless vanity? When age or disease has stopped us in our tracks, we may contemplate these questions, often too late, for we can see around the bend that the time we're given here is nearly over. I realize I have come to west Pokot to build a bridge, but now I also realize that I have left too fast from my western culture and am feasting on theirs.

We slow down as we approach another town. I hold onto the door's high grip to steady myself from the erratic turns of our vehicle, as Harmon attempts to miss the deep, five-foot wide potholes. Mud puddles from a recent rain and billows of dust rising up from where the sun has dried the earth add to Harmon's difficulty in maneuvering the Land Rover. We hold on tight. The town looks wobbly from the movement of the car, but I can still make out merchants standing in front of their shops. It appears as though they slapped together with whatever materials they could find that would ward off the heat, wind and rain, in an act of construction that comes from the union of poverty and ingenuity.

Men sit on wooden porches that remind me of the Old West, sewing on ancient looking treadle sewing machines. Dogs roam, as do the children. With baskets or plastic buckets on their heads, people are always carrying something somewhere. If their heads aren't carrying a parcel, they are adorned with a hat or a wrap. I've seen amazing hats, some I recognize as hand-me-downs from my country, and some look like Picasso has become a milliner. Our friends, Hoyt and Lois, who live in Kagundo, told us they once saw a man walking in the heat with a furry blue toilet seat cover strapped on as a hat.

My favorite hat delight was a scene of beauty. A tall, thin man, grayed at the temples, stood by the roadside. His hat caught my attention before I could even make out his features! It was something of finely crocheted cotton, dyed in earth tones. The geometric pattern on the cloth was something I thought I might see on a medieval warrior's shield and was wrapped around the high pill box shape. He looked so distinguished and proud to be alive, with a neck erect as if he was keeping watch over those around him. Shepherd-like, he scanned the road up and down like a faithful watchman. Who needs a camera? The handsome Kenyan man is part of me now, a picture I can pull up at any time, my Chief of Hats.

It is late afternoon on September 30th, elevation 6,000 feet. The air is cool in the city of Kitale. We turn down a long, dirt road lined with trees, to go through a gate that marks this place to be private and set apart. The historic Kitale Club is a golf course that was established in 1920. It is a one-story building, homely and non-descript, but like many people, once you enter in, façades lose importance, and the inner person is revealed, usually as a hidden treasure of life's experiences to enjoy. Such is the Kitale Club. The dark wooden door closes on it's own behind us, and I am trapped in the past, for nothing has changed since the 1920's. I can hardly breathe. Am I here or there? Have I entered a place in the past where my grandparents may have enjoyed the frolics of their youth, or is it really today? The ceilings are twelve feet high; the floors are made of a creaky, uneven dark wood. The center of focus is a fabulous antique oak counter with a Kenyan man standing behind it on full alert. His face says it all—a face so open, a smile so big, that I could walk right into him. Is he the hotel, the one who brings respite and safety to the traveler? His sincere warmth, a humanness I envy, is the spirit of Kenya. Words need not be spoken, but out they pour—rich, masculine, melodious, "At last you're here. We've been waiting for you. Harmon, Harmon, how have you been?"

I sense the party has begun. This is old-world hospitality at its best. I might as well be disguised as Santa Clause for the happiness I receive in just showing up. I am home, halfway around the world, and I am home. I question if someone paid for this warmth, or is it an integral part of the large black man behind the desk? In California, we train employees in gracious service, but here in Kenya, the beauty of love springs up from what family and friends have sown into their children's souls.

We peek in the adjacent room to see where the noise is coming from. Wealthy Kenyans form a horseshoe around a television with their heads tilted downward, leaning goat-like as if any minute they will butt the set. It all seems like a horrible invasion into the ambience of the evening, and we turn away quickly without exchanging a word. We go down the hallway, out into the open air patio, and then through another private-looking door. We're in a bar that overlooks the golf course. Liquors line the wall behind the bar in rows up to the ceiling. I smell the alcohol and smoke that has soaked into the walls over the years along with a pungent air of exclusivity that speaks of wealth and entitlement. I hear those voices of the past—the accent of Brits, Americans, and East Indians, and I hear the quiver in their speech as they discuss nation's problems, their life and wealth in Kenya and the threat of war. It is the ghostly voice of the past that I hear whisper in my ear, archival and permanent. It is history speaking.

Once settled in our bungalow, we can't wait to be outside again. Giant eucalyptus and juniper scar the rolling lawns with their towering trunks, creation's natural fences that make wonderful homes for monkeys and poisonous snakes. We set out for our evening walk. My lover turns to me, his chest pressing close in an unspoken plea that we are never to be separated. We kiss. A thin slice of sunlight is still left in the sky. I still want him, all is not over, only the light of this day is gone. Our hopes for tomorrow we share as we do all else. I am still infatuated by this man who has turned on the lights for me since I was nineteen, lost and in a very dim place. He has been and will always be the answer to my childlike cry for help, my protector, loyal to the core, my answer to prayer. Here with him now, I am safe.

We join Harmon for dinner in the formal dining room. I'm wearing a long, black, silk skirt, with slits up each side, a copper colored top that is wrapped several times around the shoulder with an African print kikoi shawl. I have three layers of Kenyan bead, bone and metal necklaces, beaded bracelets up my arm, and of course, large metal pounded earrings that coil into a cylinder. I feel beautiful and free. The sixties hippie inside me emerges.

I think the meal is delicious. Harmon says it is fair. We have chicken with Indian spices served on a bed of rice. I'm too tired to ask the name of the dish. After all, we've traveled far, seen three Rothschild Giraffes, exotic birds and counted twenty-one monkeys running free about the golf course.

We have also survived driving the highway. Many do not. Harmon tells us about Mt. Elgon that towers 14,000 feet into the sky. An eight mile hike up her crater top puts you where elephants safari to scrape the walls of caves for minerals. I have already started planning a trip to return and hike where the elephants roam. I've only hiked to 12,000 feet in the Colorado Rockies, high enough to know I want to go higher. Another day has passed and we are closer than ever to building our bridge.

I woke up to the sounds of birds, a musty smell that I identify as years of use, layers of furniture polish, and a fireplace where ashes still remain. I awoke to the heat which lets me know the sun has been up early, soaking up moisture anywhere it can. Harmon arrives from a friend's house where he has slept well, except for a very loud, early morning dog fight. Wild dogs form packs at night to roam the street and are considered a real threat.

We leave the Kitale Club and now get to see the people—my favorite part. A parade of people is walking or riding sidesaddle on the back-board seat of old Chinese pedal bikes. The owner of a bike pedals hard to get his passengers to their destination. There are far more Chinese bike taxis than cars that line the side of the road, rush hour style. The town has grown in the eleven years since Harmon, Teri and three-year old Joshua stepped onto its dry earth with nothing but three suitcases to their name and a love for the Kenyans that was and is so strong that they left all they had to come to serve them.

Once in the main area of town, we stop when children run to our car, faces pressed against the window, begging us for food or money. We ignore them as well as we can, but how can a grandmother possibly push them away? Sadness fills my soul. There is no choice in my response for I'm like a dry riverbed soaking up the rain as it pours down from the mountain. Sorrow streams into me as I see my grandchildren's faces in their faces. I choose to try and separate myself from the pain and compartmentalize so I can go on with the morning. Want is everywhere, so I am on a daily regimen of seeing, loving as well as I can, and letting go.

There's a big step up onto the sidewalk, and we move across the covered porch and into the grocery store that has mostly canned goods and sundries much like I've seen in a 1940's cowboy movie. There is no John Wayne behind the counter, but a smiling East Indian, or shall I say Asian, as they do here, who is a friend of Harmon's. We are all very interested in each other, so we freely exchange honest questions that some westerners you've just met might reply with, "None of your business!" Whatever pops into our minds is open game. We ask questions like, "How did you settle here? Where did you come from? Why have you stayed?" The shop owner is thrilled to talk and then fires back his questions to us. He looks around the store for a gift, and decides on a candy bar for each of us in honor of meeting friends of his dear friend, Harmon. This is just another daily reminder of how our friend Harmon, the bridge builder, captures the heart of people with his storehouse of love.

A stop for fuel on the outside of the town begins as a mundane, needed chore. I go around the back of the station to use the restroom. It is far from a rest. It is one of the filthiest restrooms I've experienced since the marketplace in Guadalajara in 1969, which left an indelible impression. When I come back to the car, Harmon is intently looking up and down the street. Seconds before, a small group of people, now several hundred, had swarmed ant-like to cover the pavement. Where did they come from, seemingly out of nowhere, and so quickly? Harmon stops the pump, turns to us with a pensive glare and says, "Let's get out of here now. A mob is forming." He's been caught in one before, engulfed by bodies, a dark cloud enveloping the car, sticks jabbed through the small slit openings of the windows. My dear friend, Dixie, Teri's mom, was in the car then, and to this day, when I hear her tell the story, I'm amazed they came out alive. One wrong turn down a street can be deadly. I wondered who prayed for their safety that frightful day. We speed up the hillside away from the angry crowd.

We're looking forward to a beautiful climb up to 7,000 feet. The mountain range is a gorgeous green that peaks and rolls into canyon-steep valleys. Off to the left, we can see into Uganda, only twenty-five miles away. Harmon tells us a story about a missionary family who lived in the most remote area of this region. One night, the father awoke to his dog barking and went to check her. A python was eating one of her puppies. He stabbed it through with a spear, sinking it far into the earth. The next morning, he came to find the snake and the spear was gone. The people in this area believe that pythons have supernatural powers. A chill goes up my spine, and I am glad I didn't hear this story at a campfire just before going to bed. It's horrifying enough to hear this story in broad daylight, with car doors locked, on our way to the land of wild elephants, leopards, Cape buffalo, and vipers. Here in Kenya, I need everything repeated twice that has any significance for it all seems to be spoken in a foreign language.

There's plenty of time to think as we're climbing up Marich Pass, behind a slow moving relief truck trudging its way up the mountain, lumbering side to side like an old, overweight woman. Slowly, she heads forward like a persistent mother toward the starving mouth of Ethiopia and Sudan.

Armed policemen stop us at a check station. After Harmon's forceful persuasion spoken in perfect Swahili tells them we can fend for ourselves against the armed bandits that have been coming out of the mountains, the police consent and let us go. We've hidden our money in different spots in the Land Rover and left enough to satisfy the robbers if they stop us. If we let the police escort us in a convoy, they drive slowly and the thieves see this as an opportunity to come down from the mountainside. If there's a shootout, one is caught in the crossfire. It is safer for us to go on our own.

We drop down the pass and head for Ortum. Without a guide, I would have passed by the settlement, for there is nothing to indicate this village except for a small, narrow dirt road to our left. The vegetation is worn off from the feet of animals and travelers who have come to the town to buy or sell their goods. Just as we slow to make a turn to the left, little faces peek from behind trees and out of hut windows. The sound of the engine brings out a ballet of tattered, dirty rags swinging in the breeze as their owners, thin as coat hangers, run to us with bare feet, billowing up puffs of dust around them. They are like a little herd of scampering waifs headed for us—the watering hole. We provide smiles, conversation and touch. They drink it up as only child-like hearts that seek out attention, stimulation, affection, and who are curious to the core can. I bask in their friendly little faces.

We pass a flat-roof hut on our left, where there is a corn grinder. The people come down from the steep mountains with a forty pound sack of corn slung on their backs to have it ground and then hopefully sold. If they cannot sell it, they climb back up the peak to their huts. I estimate they burn 10,000 calories on their day trip, who knows? The concept of dieting is absurd here in the land of survival. "Dirt poor" takes on a deeper meaning, when all you have left in life is the dirt around you from which to produce a living.

The Rafiki Hotel is only a grove of wild fig trees with weaver bird nests hanging from them, thorny bushes, and a horseshoe turn-away. Harmon has fantasized out loud about us eating together there. "Wait, wait you guys until we eat at the Rafiki Hotel in Ortum. Lynn, you could wear your pearl and silver Swahili wedding necklace. I can hardly wait for you to see it." He explained little about our luncheon date, but the excitement in his voice let us know we were in for a spectacular cultural experience. It may not be the best Beverly Hills has to offer, but I've been there, done that and it all rings a hollow toll when I hear the small voice within me question, "Is this all there is in life?"

My question is answered without a conscious thought of it when I see Rafiki's face for the first time. Weathered but majestic as all else here in west Pokot, she is an age-old building of crumpling stucco, the paint so bleached I'm unable to tell the color of her youth. Her sign is hung high above the open air walking porch. I discover it has a very important indicator of what lies within, as I read its comical title in English in this scrawny bit of a village: "Rafiki Hotel – Famous Restaurant." Famous to whom, I chuckle to myself. It's all comparison and I lay mine aside to fully appreciate Rafiki.

I've never felt, seen or smelled anything like this. It is a burning center of life for the locals, which far surpasses any Starbuck's I've ever entered. The artist within me ignites, clicking mental pictures with every blink of my eye. The people are a circus treat for us and us for them. We stare at each other, just stare. Harmon is enjoying it all and takes the lead to escort us to a table and chairs, or else I think I would have been paralyzed, turned to stone, stuck in time by the thrill of this place! The walls are a blur of turquoise and gold painted years ago. The dust and dirt of life have powdered them into an aging cracked canvas that looks like a painting of modern art, if I squint my eyes almost shut and give myself permission to walk on the wild side, to live, to imagine.

The ceiling I'd say is fifteen-feet high, so there's plenty of wall space to hold a trophy of signs and pictures. The first one to catch my eye is a picture of Saddam Hussein. Under it are bold letters "Al-Hajj, Saddam the Hero." Then there's a round metal emblem with a small arch on the top of it inscribed with "Always." In the center of the emblem it says "Coca-Cola." Behind me is a Midwestern looking print of praying hands. Where in the heck did it come from? Somali Muslims own this restaurant and they have quite an interesting choice of wall décor. The last picture I saw was of a monkey reading a newspaper. Above it says, "Don't just sit there, do something." It's a good thought for the moment so we decide to wash our hands in a sink that is near the table, shake off the water in the hot air, shoo off flies and order the only thing they have to offer – goat backbone stew, boiled potatoes, collard greens and chili sauce. I'm hungry so the stew tastes good, even though the only meat I get is the flavor of it in the sauce. Another fly lands on me, roosters crow, goats mill around in the shade and I let a fleeting thought slip in, "I wonder if I'll get food poisoning?" The thought goes with the flies and with the distraction of hearing a bad rendition of *Rock of Ages* playing on the radio.

Harmon says, "Oh good, a chief is here. We'll get some action." Two sub-chiefs of this area shake our hands and warmly greet Harmon. Swahili flows, bridge formalities are spoken about and important details agreed upon.

We walk through the arched doorway toward the car. A little boy, almost too little to catch my eye, is standing in the shade of a deserted building with his shoulders leaning against a rusted iron door much the way an old man would, one who barely had the strength to stand. His green wool sweater, a must for cold winter days was adding much too much weight and heat for his poor little frame. Barefoot and alone, we left him. All is not well with me. How can it be? All is not well with this child.

I contemplate my purpose for life and cannot escape the question—will I?

Will I ...

Will I invest my life in dead things? Materialism that feeds my insecurity and produces loss?

Will I spend my talents carelessly as if they were given to me for no lasting purpose?

> Am I to breathe and feel, to eat and play and never
> stop to give my life away?
> Will the driving force of my existence be rooted in
> God's glorious name?
> Will my life's efforts fade away as a piece of cloth in
> the hot African sun?
> Or, will they radiate Jesus, to be counted in the life
> to come?

I'm tempted to crawl into a ball, potato bug style, and spiritually fit tight into a fetal shape—self-protective and inward, the beginning of death and the exact opposite of what I have been called to do.

Forty minutes pass quickly. It's a time to think about the day and settle myself so I have emotional room to take in the late afternoon and evening ahead. We come to the turn and take a dirt road where the shoulders are covered with tall trees and deep bush. How can anyone ever find this place? It's a tunnel of green and brown camouflaged into the surroundings. The Marich Field Study Center, or as I've quickly name it, "The Resort" is an oasis constructed by the Moruny River.

An open area has been cleared for the brave who tent camp, the up-scale tourists sleep in huts that form a semicircle around the screened-in dining room. Bones, dried out and bleached by the sun's mighty rays are to be found everywhere in Kenya and act as architectural shrines that remind us of our own mortality. So stand these five-foot high elephant bones, magnificent curved lines, sculpturally perfect, placed as a greeting, a sign to show us we have arrived.

Dr. David Roden and his wife, Hidat, are the visionary force that gave birth to this little settlement, a place where people come from all over the world to do research about the west Pokot and its people, animals and land. David and Hidat have a charming story about how they came to settle here. Their unconventional hearts, crying to fulfill their own personal destiny, took the lead in their walk down the Moruny riverside. They stopped at this spot and looked up the hillside to see their dream. Ideas flooded into their minds and through providence, the Marich Field Study Center was conceived. Peace settled on them.

The sun sets quickly here at the equator. We can hear nature's residents scurry around us, as they heed the warning sign that as fast as light escapes the day, danger comes. Harmon works to set up his tent on the edge of a tree studded cliff, overlooking the river. We're told we'll hear the drums of the Pokot's as they perform a rain dance tonight. There is a drought and famine is predicted. I already think there's a famine because the people are so bone-exposing thin. I'm informed that what I see is malnutrition, whereas a famine is death.

Darkness is upon us. Bats fly overhead. The sound of distant drums mix with the constant chirp of crickets rubbing their legs together and the muffled flow of the Moruny, the river over which we've come to build a bridge. A cool breeze reaches through the Acacia trees and brings the same soothing calm that a sunset brings. The heat has gone with the daylight, and we three sit around our campfire. Harmon plays his guitar, I read my poetry, and Herb makes us laugh with his hilarious childhood stories.

Herb is a caregiver to the core. I see the silhouette of his broad shoulders, and he is bent at the waist in a servant's posture that shows me he is once again tending to the needs of others. He carefully stirs the coals to ward off the chill and make sure we have the perfect ambience. How can I ever say no to this man? He has cared and worked for me since our first dance, always looking for a way to thrill me with a surprise. Our first date was a private airplane ride in a single engine Cessna. It's been an adventure being married to such a man, and now we're on our biggest adventure of all. There's just enough light to see a white feather floating above the water, Herb says it is a good sign. I'm reminded of a poem I wrote him after a Sierra evening walk on May 6, 2001.

> *Wild Pigeon, Feathered Owl,*
> *How Rich She Really Is.*

> *The setting sun cast light below her waist so she bent over to spy a treasure. Manicured nails of peach lifted up an owl feather close to her face. The pattern of its golden, tawny strips shimmered in the twilight. Its awesome beauty captivated her. Her sight, ability to think, all mental and spiritual health focused in on a fallen feather. How she wished she could join this fleeting creature of flight, to become a feather on his wing, to fly with him and sing. To soar at night.*

> *Her love of many years said, "Here's a wild pigeon feather you might like. It's not very pretty, though." Taking the drab feather, she cherished it not for beauty's sake, but because of her mate. Late that evening, she placed the two feathers in her tin box of memories.*

> *No one knew how rich she really was. The rusted box held her thoughts of yesterday. The diamond on her finger shows society she is married, but the feathers in the box tell the story of their love together.*

Frogs croak bull-horn loud from the river. The evening has turned into a prehistoric black. We make our way to the dinner with our flashlights searching the ground left to right as if we are prison guards intently looking for escapees. We are warned that three inch thorns will go right through the soles of our shoes if stepped on, that the snakes are out and that we have about two block lengths of bush to navigate until we arrive at the dinner hut. Fear, hunger and excitement mix together. I taste them so clearly that they are my appertif.

Our meal of rice, goat, and garden vegetables is delicious. I wasn't expecting the food to be this good, nor was I expecting to be able to drink the well water. A Pokot woman lifts a large, black lantern for Herb and I to make our way to our sleeping quarters. The hut has a thick, wooden, fortress-like door that looks like it must have shrunk or maybe the person who made it miscalculated its size. Whatever the case, there is a gap at the bottom that offers enough space for almost any snake to slither into our bedroom. Harmon told us earlier of his recent stay here when a woman called for help.

David was in England so she called out for Harmon. He asked what the matter was and she said, "There's a snake in my bed." He just laughed about it. It must be the African that's grown in him over the years—laughing in the face of fear.

We're told to zip our suitcases up tight, shake out our clothes and shoes before putting them on, because of the scorpions. I add "check the bed for snakes" to the list. Our round sleeping room has two twin beds with mattresses on top of poured cement bases. A mosquito net hangs over each bed. At night, Herb meticulously tucks me in. Entombed, the net is squeezed as tight as it will go under the mattress, malaria-proof snug. I feel claustrophobic with the net so near my face and the heat of the enclosed hut causing me to sweat. I tell the child within me not to get out of bed, but I want to fly home—only for a second. At home, my biggest fright is possibly breaking a nail when I reach into my designer bag for a credit card.

A little air comes in from two very small, rectangular, port-hole windows near the ceiling. Africans don't like windows, but I'm sure leopards do. There are beetles and a spider in our room that runs so fast, Herb has given up any attempt to kill him. My conscious mind begins to fade into the night when I hear Herb yell, "What's that? What's that?" The hunter in him poised. "There it is again, a bat." It flies back and forth in the black of night from its nest in the center peak of our hut, into the bathroom and back again. I've never heard Herb say "Oh, shit" so many times, but I realize it's his way to deal with the fact that he is sleeping in the same room with a bat. My way of handling the situation is to joke. I warn Herb, "Be sure not to step in bat pee and pooh when you get out of bed tonight to go to the toilet." The next morning at breakfast, Herb tells Hidat that there is a bat in our room. She looks at him with a smile of sublime acceptance and replies, "Well, after all, this is Africa." We all laugh.

What was it that awoke me this morning? Was it the heat, the bush alive with the chatter of monkeys competing with birds in concerto or the growing excitement in me to see the bridge site for the first time? Mosquito net pushed aside, and my pants pulled on, I walk to the river. It is 7:00 am and the new day blisters with heat. What will it be like at noon?

A Pokot man crosses the water with his walking stick to help him balance on the exposed river stones, his machete reflecting the eastern sun like a Star Wars light saber. His lean, red dog turns to show his white face. It looks healthy and loved, the first I've seen like this in the Pokot. A woven blanket, various shades of dirt, is draped over his one hand, around his shoulder and to his knee the tip dangles. A bag is slung from his shoulder, swinging as he and his fox-like dog disappear between the trees. No one but the sun and I have seen him start his day. Something in me cries, "Don't leave, let me go with you." Intimacy at its best, he is my waking hours' delight, my entry into the day.

I'm silent about the man and dog as we congregate outside the dining hut on the patio overlooking the river at a distance. Hidat's helper has delighted us with her daily chore of roasting coffee beans over an open fire, grinding them and then pouring hot water over the grounds, resulting in a dynamite strong demitasse of Ethiopian coffee. The process takes about forty-five minutes. No rush hour traffic to worry about, we watch her with the enjoyment that is ours to be had each day, but that is robbed us by hectic schedules, self-imposed rituals, and skewed priorities. One blink and life is over. When did we forget to enjoy life? What blinded us from seeing the beauty that is in each day?

I have porridge and eggs. It is our last meal until late evening, just as the people here exist. David apologizes for his lethargy, which I haven't noticed, and says he's been feeling a bit malarias. It comes on him several times a year. He tells us the local news. Recently, David's toilet cleaner drank moonshine made from yellow corn and it paralyzed him. He was taken off in a wheelbarrow. The table is quiet, except for the elephants that can be heard across the river, eating woody brush. David says we won't see them. I ask if there are crocodiles in the river. In a monotone, he replies, "Only small ones, about the length of this table. No one here has been hurt, but they have been upstream." I start to eat again, camouflaging my shock to think eight-foot crocodiles living where I went to meditate this morning, by the river's edge.

Our conversation turns to faith. Hidat looks at Herb, pauses and then breathes out one of her glorious proverblike statements, "Herb, you always remember God. If you remember him," pointing her finger from her heart and then to heaven, "you will never fail." There is finality to her words, our signal that it is time to head toward our future bridge.

Ortum is our first stop, which we need to make for fuel. A sign hanging above a shed reads, "Ngasian Women Group Filling Station, Petrol Station, PO Box 8, Ortum." Agnes, one of the female entrepreneurs, runs the gas station. Glaring into the sun that beats into her eyes, she comes from behind Herb, points to his sunglasses, and asks if he has any goggles. By chance, he has brought six pairs from his industrial safety equipment business and looks into his bag to retrieve a pair for her. Long hours in the glaring sun must have taken its toll on her. She thanks us over and over again.

A little boy who looks to be about four years old stands a few feet behind her, with one foot in a green plastic bucket to steady it as he washes his blue rubber flip flop sandals with an old corn cob. His striped shirt hangs to his thighs. Getting the correct size of clothing is not the issue, the concern is just having something to cover you. The little boy is happy and busy, just like my grandsons when they have a "big boy" chore to do. He waves his wet hand at us and says proudly in English, "How are you?" I smile and say, "Fine." Then, as if I'm his English teacher, I repeat his phrase, "How are you?" He is thrilled to practice his English and says, "Fine." We pull away with my hand waving to him out the window, as he stands in the mud of his work puddle, frantically waving his arms back and forth at me with his frail body swaying from side to side like a flag in the wind.

There's a joy in him that comes from simplicity. Things are slow enough in his world that he is able to smell the essence of life in the air, and human encounters are precious. No waking early, no rush to eat, dress and strap into a car seat for a commute to preschool for this young one. He has little food, scanty clothes, no toys, no car, or school, but he has a smile that says, "Whoever you are, I welcome you." Undistracted by television, computers, or video games, there is an uncluttered spirit in him that makes room for everyone he sees. This brief encounter has taught me well. My primary lesson for the day is to enjoy the simplest task and to honor others.

We travel less than half an hour, with every scene presenting itself as a story to be written, a tender picture of Pokot life viewed through my internal window. I've lost track of time in the land of few watches. The timepiece I have now is watching, seeing others without the thought of time.

I'm amused at a culture that esteems modesty, yet the men bathe on one side of the river in full view of the women, who bathe on the opposite side. They have no thought of nudity, for they are busy getting clean, drying themselves and wrapping their bodies in cloth.

We make a sharp left turn off the main road, to a steep mountain ascent, missing holes and maneuvering around boulders and trees. This is the pathway the people have cleared for us to drive as far as possible with Harmon's supplies. I'm laughing, while I hold on for dear life. Harmon grips the wheel of his bucking bronco and jerks it to the left before we're thrown off the hillside. Swerving back to the right to miss a tree, his engine revs to conquer the incline. I'm seeing flashes of green foliage, man-sized rocks, and my life passing before me. The laughter has stopped to give me room to just breathe. Once at the top, Harmon stops and turns to us, "Pretty good road. Pretty good. Not as bad as some I've been on. You should have seen the one at the very top of the mountain." He's serious. I'm glad that part of the journey is over, but hope it's not a foreshadowing of the day ahead.

When the road becomes totally impassable, we stop and get out. It feels so good to let my equilibrium rest. At first, the only two people I see are a woman bending over at the waist to pick up a wet mixture of cow dung and earth that she uses to repair the outer walls of her hut. Her baby, maybe a year old, plays in the dirt, where I think she is dangerously far from her mother. She seems to be enjoying her work and I immediately relate to her as my friend, another woman I'd call to say, "Hey, I'm faux painting my dining room walls today. Would you like to come over and help? Then we can go for lunch." She sees me smiling at her and comes down switch-back style on the slope with her baby now on her hip. We visit with smiles and sign language. I coo over her baby, who has the sweetest little munchkin face. Children appear from nowhere. We are like the toy magnets of my childhood, we the white Scotty dogs, they the black. Placed near each other, the pull of curiosity plus the human desire of closeness causes a draw that throws race aside, a force so strong it must come from the hand of our Creator.

Everyone but me picks up supplies. All the men, American and Kenyan, insist I carry nothing. I stop my protest quickly when I see their honor for age and a need to have a queen accompany them. We walk the narrow goat trail, leaning into the mountain's shoulder when it gets so narrow that we can only place one foot directly in front of the other, tightrope style.

Sylvester Ouko Odudr, Harmon's paid helper, carries three men's share with his lean muscle-of-a-body. Harmon tells us that Sylvester rides his gearless pedal bicycle twenty miles to a neighboring town, up and down the steep mountains and then back home again. He looks ten years younger than his true age of thirty-five. He is very handsome, witty and energetic, especially when telling us Bible stories. Since we met him early this morning, I've heard all about Moses and Noah. He shares his stories enthusiastically, as one might share the plot of a new movie he has just seen. The fact that we might already know the story isn't a consideration for him; it's the joy of sharing with us that fuels his story-telling. Story-telling is his prized possession, spoken in English with a Kenyan accent, with descriptions only one who has lived a life-time in Kenya could come up with.

Freddie, the other paid helper is quiet. With his eyes half open, he roams the landscape James Dean style, only he lives in a body that is several shades darker than the American actor.

Freddie is lean, angular and strong. There are very few words spoken by him, caused either by his appre-hension or by being a male who finds great security in being an analytical observer. I can almost touch the frag-ile gentleness buried deep within him, a non-judgmental, questioning attitude that causes us to open our hearts to him as we would to a prepubescent child. He is disarm-ing and cautiously polite. I wonder what he has heard or seen of Caucasians that causes him to be so tentative. Or is it in general what he has heard and seen, growing up in Kenya? Wary, but confident, he gently pushes the branches aside for us, so as not to create a sound. Like a leopard on the prowl, he seems invisible, but is as clear as my hand that is in front of me.

The sound I hear most often from him is his laugh. It is usually instigated by his childhood friend, Sylvester. Everything Sylvester does is the opposite of Freddie's re-serve. Sylvester is Freddie's counter-part, his alter ego. They are co-workers, best friends and never would there be a doubt that either one would immediately lay down their life for the other. I study these African men who are survivors, mighty warriors of life with playful childlike spirits. May I learn well from them even as I learn from every moment that I am in this foreign land.

We follow the red dirt path through the bush, and duck under branches. We are an unlatched necklace of people, knotted together by a common purpose—to build a bridge that will save lives and take hours off of travel time for the villagers, when the river is too swollen to cross by foot. Everyone, even little children with babies strapped on their backs, want to help. They carry water, cables, tools, expectations and love that helps carry us forward, along with the ever-present assurance of the treasured prayers being spoken on our behalf, halfway around the world.

I'm in the home of puff adders, which are snakes that curl into balls which can easily be mistaken for rocks. The prayers are working to push my snake phobia down far enough so that I can see over my fear in order to view the new day.

Down the mountain that cradles the Moruny River, along the sandy shore and passing under the welcome shade of a fig tree, we reach the bridge site. It's a beautiful spot that offers a view up the canyon until all you can see is the blue sky bordered by mountain peaks. Harmon has already been at work so the bridge can be finished in a few days. He has previously set the posts in concrete and the bare cables have been strung across the river to be anchored on each side.

I encounter a big surprise! Harmon has the posts painted orange, and unknown to him, orange is my favorite color. The Kenyan people also love the color and ask if their future bridges could be painted in the same way. Supplies are dropped and the work begins quickly; we are in a race to beat the heat.

Men from a village that will use the bridge once it is finished are straggling into the work site to help, along with more tentative-faced children that have heard news of the construction. It's an eerie feeling to see them wander in from the farthest reaches of society—pitiful, beautiful little creatures, who are the dirtiest children I have ever seen. Some of them have the white spots of malnutrition on their scalps, accompanied by a lifeless glare, pensive, stoic, and rooted in deprivation. The children sit down on fallen logs near the bridge supplies, and do not talk, but sit as quietly as little birds on a line. They are exhausted by the sheer survival presented by living each day in the west Pokot.

I see two women with a group of children across the river and feel a pull to be with them. Harmon says, "Sure, it'll be safe. Sylvester will take you to a shallow place to cross." The path takes us into thick bush. My story-teller guide and I are alone on a mountain trail, ducking, bending and walking sideways to avoid getting scraped by the thorny bushes. A herd of goats and a few sheep walk slowly ahead of us. Sylvester hurries them on in a commanding, high pitched yell, "Quick, quick, sheep and goats, quick, quick." The call with its meter must have come from his childhood. The goats run ahead and we wade across the river at a low spot, knee- deep, with Sylvester holding my hand to steady me from the uneven bottom. I feel a twinge of guilt as I remember the nurse at the San Jose Health Department giving us strict instructions about Kenya as freely as she administered our shots. In a very serious tone she said, "Remember, never get into the water, it is extremely contaminated." The new shore was well worth the possibility of disease to get a chance to sit with the women. The children giggle, a baby cries and then all is quiet as I approach. I walk right up and sit next to an old grandmother who is blind in one eye. She spits and the hot wind carries it close to me. They've picked a shady, sloping area under a large fig tree to sit, as it is in direct eye shot of the bridge building. I put my kikoi wrap on the damp earth to sit on and pull out my knitting from my backpack.

Handwork is our common ground. The younger woman watches me knit. I watch her weave a basket by wetting a reed in her mouth and using a wooden handled awl to loosen her previous stitch and pull the reed over and through the basket side. The basket is the size of two hands cupped together, a dark, meticulously woven piece of art. I'd love to buy it from her, half-finished, to be able to show others the process of her weaving and to pay her very well. I'll ask Ambassador Harmon about it later. He'll know the protocol.

A young girl slips a crying baby off her back and pours Chai from a small gourd into the baby's mouth. The tea streams in a steady flow from the gourd about ten inches from the baby's lips. Everyone watches the baby choking with its head held back to be an open target for the tea. No fondling or sucking for this baby, only a little mother-girl trying her best to do the job of an adult. The baby stops his gurgling and is slipped back into the back sling with only a t-shirt on, no diapers and no nappy. When he messes the back of the little girl's back, she goes down into the stream to clean herself and her bundle by dipping in the water. The other two women have watched the choking-feeding time but have not spoken a word. I interpret their body language as saying, "This is some-thing she's going to have to figure out. It's her job; we can't do it for her." There's a calm resolve in this land where AIDS and disease take so many parents, leaving the young to care for the younger. The pain I feel is so unexplainable, so inexpressible that I retreat into my role of observer in an attempt to keep from absorbing so much pain that I can't go on.

The wind is strong, and dries my tired, late after-noon body. The second dog fight of the day on the banks of the Moruny is a vicious one. I've named the contes-tants Ali and Midnight, each weighing in at about thirty pounds. First the barking, then the snarling teeth and fi-nally the rip of flesh. Blood spurts up high against the clear blue sky and then the yelps of pain cut through the silence. Ali has won both fights and stands firmly in his space. Midnight, bent over, limps toward us. The children throw stones at him in fear. He yelps louder, as if to say painfully, "From my own kind, I can take a fight, but humans, humans have the capacity to comfort me." Head down, he hobbles to a high rock cliff not far from us. Poor Midnight, defeated again. I feel sorrow for him, alone and rejected by those from whom he sought help.

Isolation
We fight, we lose, and still injured, others stone us with their words. Alone and limping from our wounds, we hurt in silence. Void of comfort, we heal slowly, if we heal at all. Only Christ, the balm of Gilead, the keeper of our souls can heal us and save us from this deadly cycle of pain.

The work day with its methodical back-bending labor in the sun, along with the drama of the dog fights is over. The men are tired but express fulfillment from their long day's work. We hike out of the canyon and once seated in the close confines of the car, I say, "Oh, I smell like a donkey." Harmon laughs and says, "No, you smell like a goat." Now I know the damp ground I sat on along with the berry pods scattered around are not exactly as it appeared. My lesson for the day is, "Don't camp where the goats romp or you'll smell like a swamp." My new official name is Princess Mbuzi, Swahili for goat. I put myself last on the list for a cold shower but the heat and the goats have changed my mind.

Light is leaving us quickly. Our hut is dim, so I shower in a hurry, while Herb unsuccessfully tries again to kill the persistent bathroom spider. A glow of light reaches its friendly hand under our door. Hidat's helper has left us a kerosene lantern to swing our way to dinner in the African darkness.

Close together, closer than we've ever been, it seems the years have escaped us it seems as quickly as the evening light. We hold hands and walk to dinner to the sounds of crickets and the last sharp call of a bird. Our lantern sways back and forth, spreading light with a slow rhythm as if we were aboard a ship, adrift at sea, alone in a universe of darkness.

We scan the night. I recall the past and know Herb has definitely fulfilled his promise to me when he said in a seductive whisper in my ear, "Marry me and I'll take you traveling." At first it was in a Volkswagen bus. Barely able to afford the gas, we'd head toward the Mendocino Coast to roam the beaches and kiss the way only lovers can under the passion of the moon. All the while, hardship, disappointment, the joy of children, illness, Bay Area stress, a business run and now sold, our romance has not only survived, but has triumphed over all.

From the black of night, we enter a large hut with white walls glaring at us with a ceremonial purity. The only furniture is a long table with chairs and a row of black iron lanterns pouring out light down the center of the table. The clean white walls seem like intruders or a color from another planet after being in the dirt of the bush all day. Hannah and Vanessa enter the room. They accessorize this space that is void of pictures, figurines, and candles, and is as bleak as a hospital room.

These two brave women have traveled from England to study the Pokot's perception of malaria. They go into the most remote villages on the elephant side of the river with a pen, a notebook and an interpreter to conduct thirty or more interviews. They ask questions like, "Why do you think you get malaria?" Some think it comes from eating Western food or sweets. The women tell us the effects of drought are harrowing. One village has lost two hundred goats in the last eighteen months. They've seen people who haven't eaten in days. The experience has dimmed the glimmer in their eyes, but they are still able to put away the knowledge of the villager's plight and join in with us to enjoy being together with us.

Harmon has arrived from his campsite. He's bathed with a stone for lack of soap. David and Hidat enter the room joyously, the food carried procession-style behind them with a medieval flare. Our conversation is as delectable as the food, as it stretches from politics to faith to geography and then to the topic of the treacherous road we traveled to get here.

A lone tear of sorrow runs down Hidat's face as she tells us of a friend who was killed while driving back to Nairobi. The loss is fresh. The damage is real. Likewise, David shares about an old man who worked for them. They dearly loved him and when he didn't show up for work one day, or the next, a party was sent out to his village to check on him. His remains (or what was left of them) were found, and it was apparent that he had suffered a Cape buffalo attack. I'm so glad they've shared their stories of loss and have let us into their sacred room, the room of grief, which others often keep locked and bolted. There are no apologies for tears or sadness, only two dear people being vulnerable in the land where life and death greet you daily.

Dinner is over, and we retire early with the thought of a big day before us. Herb tucks my mosquito net in around me and puts the smelly kerosene lantern outside our door. Its light slips gracefully under our door, and is hopefully not followed by a reptile. Herb's cold is an annoying presence with us as he coughs day and night. His phlegm, which was a clear, bright orange while we were in Nairobi, has now turned into an infectious green. He ignores it, fighting his ground to conquer sickness. I have had bad cactus throat for three days. I think it is from the drought and not a virus.

When have I slept like this? The night so silent that thick heat still rests on me like a heavy blanket. I must be in a dehydrator, coming out in the morning as a little prune of a person. A gut prayer emerges from me over-riding all else:

Take me to a place native and wild where the thrill of living each day comes first in the bursting sunrise. The awe of seeing the unknown, the pull of hardship that stretches my spiritual muscle—give me, if You will, a view of my life compared to others, so that in comparison, I might see more clearly. May I live the life of a tigress in the land of emerald green, able to know the prey, to attain wisdom and to conquer, even if the enemy is within, myself. Amen.

My prayers, the heat and my thoughts of life gone by fill the restless night.

I awake in a semi-comatose state with a sore throat and water the only thing I desire. "Who cares?" I think, "I'm still in Africa." Our door is open for ventilation and a Verbit monkey interrupts my first pee of the day. I jump off the black toilet seat to chase him away.

Rain came during the night but the overzealous morning sun has already sucked up the moisture around our hut. The foliage of the acacia fern keeps the sun from overpowering our doorway. Her twisted branches writhe like restless snakes uncoiling toward the daylight for a morning stretch. Everything is alive and moving. There is a quiver of electricity in the air around me as if everything has had one too many cups of coffee.

Breakfast is served on the patio "crocodile table" as I've named it since only the small croc, the eight-foot length of this table, lives in the river near us. My mind drifts from dangerous nearby creatures to the smell of food. We are served porridge, sliced mango, honey with corn cakes, eggs, bacon with sautéed tomato and the famous Ethiopian coffee. Vanessa, who wants to bring home some honey, says in her English accent, "The way they sling suitcases at the airport—no." I can see the suitcases "slinging" Frisbee-style and sailing shoulder-high through the luggage claim area. Everything amuses me today: the flute call of a bird, Vanessa's choice of words and the sight of myself in a mirror.

My eye catches the sight of a leaf floating across the crude field study center road, leading out to the main road. There's a half acre garden to the right and I see somewhere in the distance of my daydream, a journal opened to today. Its thin parchment lays open and is bare except for one word written in script so beautifully that I squint to decipher what appears to be holy and make out a single scroll of a word, a title for the day: "Destiny."

This picture sticks in my mind as clearly as the hillside woman we saw when Harmon took us to one of his bridges. She had come down from a drastically steep switchback path. She stood on the hillside of the bridge holding a walking stick and wearing a colorful crocheted cap pulled snug to her scalp. It was difficult to tell her age. At home, I pride myself in the art of guessing people's ages, but here, the elements of weather, food or the lack thereof, and disease rob me of my skill. I'm left loosely, as all judgment should be, to a generalization. She must be the honored one, the survivor, the oldest person I've seen here. I try to imagine myself without a dentist or a hair colorist, without makeup or facial creams, and sleeping in a smoke-filled hut, living my days out in the sun, wind, and rain. What I envision is not a pretty picture, but she, the hillside woman, is wonderfully aged to perfection.

We stare at each other. The bridge Harmon has built lies between us, and is a passageway we dare not cross in fear of scaring her away. She throws her leather cape into the air behind her and then quickly sits on it like a sofa cover that comes between her and the earth. With the cape aside, I see how fashionably thin she is, the curve of muscle is still in her lean arms. Her high cheekbones mirror the jagged rocks that hold the mountain back from falling fifty feet into the Moruny. I say, "Is that an incredible cape!" Harmon brings definition, "It's made of aardvark skin, very rare."

The woman is pensive and as quiet as a turkey hunter waiting in early morning light for any movement, any sign of a feather from her prey. Harmon says, "Herb, she can't get her eyes of your neon yellow shirt. A color I'm sure she has never seen. She's tripping on it." His terminology from our past brings definition to the present. We are "tripping" on each day. The Beetles' lyrics play in my mind: *"Day tripper, it took me so long to find out ..."* We are not the yesterday of our youth but the today of our near sixties, the present that holds hope and vision. The best is yet to come.

A drive, a hike and now I am again at the bridge site. The men work hard to construct the bridge and ward off the heat. The toothless grandmother with ragged, torn ears is here again. I go to be with her and this time there is no spitting. She may be getting used to me. I study her ears to see if I can tell if they came by way of a ritual, by a hyena attack, or maybe a violent grab to steal her earrings. The long-necked younger woman, whose hair is cropped so closely I can see her scalp, greets me with a smile and then goes back to weaving her basket. There is nothing stale or tasteless in this exchange of women greeting other women.

Gnats swirl about us, flies land, and only the Lord knows whatever insects crawl around us. The children form a double, uneven dark chocolate wall behind me. I hear them play and cough. Any time I catch their eye, they smile. About mid-day, the woman and children leave, ascending up the mountain trail that is so steep I can only see them for a few moments before they disappear into the twisted bush, as if they've walked into the jaws of some unnamed giant, never to be seen again.

The sky darkens after they leave. It's as if they sense the storm as easily as they breathe the air. Alone on the bank, easy prey, maybe just for my own fears, I cross the low waters, walk down the sheep and goat rut to the bridge site. Welcomed moisture, a witch's cauldron of darkness comes brewing down the canyon. The pot boils over within a few minutes and is followed by the overflowing downpour that comes when a slice has been made into heaven. The rain pours. Everyone huddles under trees. I scramble for my three dollar poncho, as does Herb. The water runs down my sloping, hunched shoulders like I am the face of a dam. Everyone else is soaked but us. They shiver and laugh while shaking off the cold in the same resistant, victorious attitude that permeates their lives.

The once placid river swells to a muddy chocolate brown torrent and carries tree branches down its rapids. Herb and I get to see first-hand how quickly a storm can come and leave cold, wet, hungry people on the bank, stranded sometimes for several days.

The rain subsides. Children straddle the coals from a small fire. All get back to work, ignoring the fact that they are soaked through and slipping into the gummy mud. The bridge is finished by late afternoon. Little children, still wet, one by one cross the river safely, high above the water's roar. The future follows them—a dark young beautiful pregnant woman is the first adult to cross. In the worst of storms or blistering heat, villages are now connected to schools, hospitals, church and trade.

The bridge built to communicate Christ's love for the Pokot's in a practical way, has left an indelible print

71

on the landscape of my soul. As we left, I turned to view the bridge one last time in hopeful prayer that someday, Kathryn's sons will visit the bridge built in honor of their mother and I think, as I turn to climb the muddy path, "If there's any hidden passion or dormant seeds of art or buried compassion lying deep within you, Africa will reach in to dislodge them and extract the finest from your being."

Leaving the bridge site triggers within me a strange sense of loss. It brings me back to Kathryn's last day. I remember waking about two in the morning. It was a date of ironic importance, July 2nd, the day I gave birth to our only daughter, Heather.

Kathryn's house was empty except for me and the happy photographs of a family that loves each other. Ron, Kathryn's husband, along with Aunt Betty was spending the night at the hospital. The boys, Zachery and Micah were staying with friends. They had made their last hospital visit to see their mom only days ago. Micah, the youngest, crawled under the hospital bed and wouldn't come out. His words still cling to me, "I'm not leaving my mommy. I'm not leaving my mommy." It brings tears to me now to think of the pain that comes when a child loses his mother. This pain is sadly repeated over and over again in Kenya, a land of far too many orphans.

The house is totally dark, but my eyes adjust quickly to tell me I am alone in Kathryn's bed, away from my immediate family and friends. Separation takes on a deeper meaning.

I reached to turn on the night light and fumble for my pen and notebook. The words came so easily, it was as if I was taking dictation. I had written a description of my cousin, a tribute to her life—so finely, so zestfully lived. The tribute complete, I immediately fell back asleep feeling drained and satisfied. It was the written words, the act of journaling that brought me such welcome sleep.

A friend of Kathryn's drove me to the hospital that morning. We commented how Kathryn made such a big deal about each person who would come to visit her in the hospital. Her southern hospitality, like an expensive perfume lingered in the air long after she was unable to communicate.

We laughed to think that her favorite red lipstick, purchased at the Dallas Neiman Marcus, had to be applied before she greeted each new guest. My job was to check to see that none had smeared onto her front teeth. That vibrant red lipstick framed her smile perfectly, like an open door that led you into the richness of her heart.

Late that afternoon, finality came. Even though we all knew the end was near, there were tears of shock, tears of loss and tears of relief that Kathryn's heroic fight was over. It was then that Betty asked me to read my tribute of Kathryn's life to the hospital staff. They huddled close to us to hear about the woman, the tender kindergarten teacher, the ailing patient who had become their friend.

The Tribute:
Scattered Seeds of Beauty
They streamed in, a myriad of people, an army of friends bearing gifts of flowers, food and cherished stories of remembrance. They brought laughter with them and tender moments they recount and hold carefully, close to them as one would hold a newborn infant.

Kathryn lay in bed and received each friend with her usual gracious, attentive ear turned toward their hearts. In perfect character, she gave back to them a portion of herself.

Each person left fuller and more settled into the reality of her parting. They savored once again her broad, welcoming smile, the beauty of her loving eyes, the joy of her laughter and most of all, the well of faith that watered her every word.

Our Texas rose, as a flower retains its fragrance. Even as its petals fall, there is a sweetness in the air around her. It speaks out, "Here is a gentle peacemaker."

Like the glow of sunlight that lingers in the sky after the great globe has made its slip behind the horizon, so Kathryn's countenance warms and awes us.

Twilight has come. The day has arrived for Kathryn Marie Krajca to join her father, sister and those she dearly loves. They're surrounded by the only One who holds her thoughts, stores her hopes and dreams in His sacred vial, her Redeemer. With outstretched arms, she joins her Savior.

Her new home prepared, Jesus is waiting for his saint. The kind counselor, loving wife and mother, precious daughter and faithful friend is now clothed in Heaven's bliss.

Her beauty, like scattered seed is now planted in our hearts.

Kathryn's Crossing is a life, a loss, a hope, and an adventure. All culminate into one incredible journey ending with a bridge built in Africa.

EPILOGUE

It's a clear warm January day in California. The eastern morning sun travels right through the sheer petals of even the most vibrantly colored Iceland poppies and throws jagged spear-like shadows onto our pebbled patio. It seems like such a dramatic Kenyan-way to begin the day with sun and its light changing the way we perceive the simplest forms of nature. Herb stands in the far corner of the yard, unaware that I'm fixated on him with his large pruning shears hanging from his hand as if they are exhausted from the work he's already put them through. The day has just begun for them and his avid gardening.

The grandfather clock ticks. I hear myself sigh like my grandmother used to and I always wondered why. My stomach growls while all else is silent except my invading thoughts. An inner freight train comes barreling down on me, a powerful explosion of sounds of wildlife, mingled with the smells of people working to survive, fragrant blossoms and rotting hummus. The scenes of Africa rush before me blocking out all else that seems so mundane. We are imprisoned by so much in our life, our hurry, locked in, doors shut and windows closed.

We are isolated by the rush we've created, bound by our own agendas and shackled by our fears. Knotted in a fist, we try to empower ourselves by bringing value to what we secretly know is all meaningless without God. Crammed full, always trying to accomplish, but what do we achieve?

Today time is moving a bit slower. Life moves on as if our trip had never happened, as if it were a figment I had wished upon myself. The morning light shining through the sheer petals of our Iceland poppies, their vibrant, primary colors so strong they help to wake me up, the scratching sound of our brownie bird who comes every morning to forage beneath our bush cherry, all these gifts from nature have stirred the memory of Africa within me.

I envision the Dark Continent as a large stone lying in a barren field. It marks what comes before it and what lies ahead. I have been given a new reference point, a just weight shall I say, to examine what I know as western reality. Often I recline near this stone and ponder what I see in Saratoga, the height of Silicon Valley success, the sought-after place to live. My stone is a place to stop and measure my daily reality. Thoughts of Africa are my rest time. Much of my anxious striving was left in the mountainous region of west Pokot, yet I still feel as if I'm dangling between two worlds. One hand holds onto the tip of Africa, another grasps the coast of California. I have become a bridge suspended between two cultures. Stretched by the knowledge I have acquired, I redefine terms like hardship, doing without, sacrifice and need.

I am in our garden where the clouds are low, the air is sweet with moisture and the Oregon juncos hop. I now see the things around me more clearly for I am looking with a new vision—through the eyes of Africa.

Roslyn, Teri's helper showers Lynn with love
and prayers of safety as the team leaves for the west Pokot.

Harmon is finishing his work on Kathryn's Crossing while I test it out.

Lined up to have their picture taken, these little ones
live in one of the poorest regions of Kenya, the west Pokot.

The children of the west Pokot will now have a safe way
to cross the river going to school and to the small hospital.
Many drownings will be prevented.

Herb crosses the completed bridge as did the villagers
later that afternoon. They needed it to get home that night
because of the heavy rain which caused the river to flood.

Lynn buys a basket from a Pokot woman that she spent the day with.
Harmon said the woman will be able to feed her family
for a week with the money.

The bridge is completed and Kathryn must be leaning down from heaven's heights enjoying it all. Joy and satisfaction at its best.

Herb with his good friend Harmon Parker, who has built over fifty foot-bridges for the Kenyans. God bless him.

Harmon and his lovely wife Teri
enjoy an evening together.

Herb and I on a two week hiking safari in Tanzania.

A view of the Rift Valley in Tanzania.

Our hiking safari took us to visit the Hadza people in Tanzania.

We were one of the fortunate five groups of people
who get to visit the Hadza people each year.

A Tompson's Gazelle is surprised by our Land Rover.

An elephant comes uncomfortably close to us.

This giraffe was raised by the Kenyans
after it's mother was killed by lions.

The baby giraffe stares at us without an ounce of fear.

David and Hidat's beloved worker was killed
by a Cape buffalo similar to this old bull.

Waterbucks are an African antelope
that live near rivers and watering holes.

Wind swept as the sun is setting on our evening game drive.

The children of Marich Pass Field Studies Centre
line up for school.

(The center is located in West Pokot, Kenya)

Ron, Kathryn and their sons, Zachery and Micah,
enjoy a family vacation in Colorado.

My Aunt Betty, always helping, took this photograph
which is now a treasure from the past.

Printed in the United States
123311LV00002B/1-276/P

9 781935 125099